MALTA

Travel Guide 2024 - 2025

The Ultimate Resource for Itineraries, Transportation, Where to Stay, What to See, Where to Eat, and Insider Tips.

Sandi H. Newman

Copyright © 2024 Sandi H. Newman. All rights reserved. No part of this publication may be reproduced, distributed, or transmitted in any form or by any means, including photocopying, recording, or other electronic or mechanical methods, without the prior written permission of the author, except in the case of brief quotations embodied in critical reviews and certain other noncommercial uses permitted by copyright law.

Disclaimer

The information contained in this book is for general informational purposes only. While the author has made every effort to ensure the accuracy and completeness of the information provided, we make no representations or warranties of any kind, express or implied, about the accuracy, reliability, suitability, or availability with respect to the book or the information, products, services, or related graphics contained in the book for any purpose. Any reliance you place on such information is therefore strictly at your own risk.

The author will not be liable for any false, inaccurate, inappropriate, or incomplete information presented in this book. The author will not be liable for any damages of any kind arising from the use of this book, including but not limited to direct, indirect, incidental, punitive, and consequential damages.

The author does not assume and hereby disclaims any liability to any party for any loss, damage, or disruption caused by errors or omissions, whether such errors or omissions result from negligence, accident, or any other cause.

All information is provided "as is" with no guarantee of completeness, accuracy, timeliness, or of the results obtained from the use of this information, and without warranty of any kind, express or implied, including, but not limited to warranties of performance, merchantability, and fitness for a particular purpose.

This book includes links to other websites for informational purposes only. These links do not signify an endorsement of the content or opinions contained within those websites. The author has no control over the nature, content, and availability of those sites.

Travel information such as visa requirements, transportation schedules, prices, and business operations are subject to change and may vary. It is recommended that travelers verify such information independently.

Any product names, logos, brands, and other trademarks or images featured or referred to within this book are the property of their respective trademark holders. These trademark holders are not affiliated with the author, and they do not sponsor or endorse this book.

The author reserves the right to make changes or updates to the content of this book at any time without prior notice.

By using this book, you agree to the terms of this disclaimer. If you do not agree with any part of this disclaimer, do not use this book.

TABLE OF CONTENTS

INTRODUCTION 6
CHAPTER 1 10
DISCOVERING MALTA 10
    The History of Malta 10
    The Maltese Culture and Traditions 14
    The Best Time to Visit Malta 18
CHAPTER 2 22
PRACTICAL INFORMATION 22
    Accommodations: Where to Stay 22
    Safety Tips and Emergency Contacts 44
    Money Matters: Currency and Budgeting 48
CHAPTER 3 52
TOP ATTRACTIONS 52
    Valletta: The Capital City 52
    Mdina: The Silent City 56
    Gozo Island: A Natural Paradise 59
    Comino and the Blue Lagoon 63
    The Megalithic Temples 66
CHAPTER 4 72
HIDDEN GEMS 72
    Off the Beaten Path: Secret Beaches 72

Quaint Villages to Explore 75
Local Markets and Artisanal Shops 79
Unforgettable Views: Hidden Lookouts 83
CHAPTER 5 88
LOCAL INSIGHTS 88
Food and Drink: Must-Try Dishes 88
Festivals and Events to Experience 91
Language and Customs 95
CHAPTER 6 104
MALTA FOR DIFFERENT TRAVELERS 104
Malta for Solo Tourists 104
Malta for Couples 108
Malta for Families 113
Malata for Groups 117
CHAPTER 7 124
USEFUL INFORMATION 124
Useful Applications for Tourists in Malta 124
Tourist Information centers in Malta 128
CONCLUSION 134

INTRODUCTION

This guide is designed to be your trusted companion as you explore the beautiful islands of Malta. Nestled in the heart of the Mediterranean, Malta is a remarkable destination known for its rich history, stunning landscapes, and vibrant culture.

Malta is made up of three main islands: Malta, Gozo, and Comino. Each island has its unique charm and offers something special for every traveler. Malta, the largest island, is where you will find the capital city of Valletta, a UNESCO World Heritage site known for its impressive architecture and historical significance. The city is a treasure trove of museums, palaces, and fortifications, all of which tell the story of Malta's diverse past. As you wander through its narrow streets, you will come across stunning views of the harbor, lively cafes, and vibrant markets, creating an atmosphere that is both welcoming and exciting.

In contrast, Gozo is a quieter island known for its breathtaking natural scenery and relaxed pace of life. Here, you can explore lush countryside, ancient temples, and beautiful beaches. The Azure Window, a famous natural arch, once stood here, drawing visitors to its stunning backdrop before it collapsed in 2017. Even without this iconic landmark, Gozo remains a haven for outdoor enthusiasts and those seeking tranquility away from the busier tourist spots.

Comino, the smallest of the three islands, is famous for its crystal-clear waters and the stunning Blue Lagoon. This idyllic spot is perfect for swimming, snorkeling, or simply soaking up the sun on the sandy beach. With limited accommodation options, Comino offers a peaceful escape from the hustle and bustle of everyday life, making it a popular day trip destination for those staying on Malta and Gozo.

The history of Malta is a captivating journey through time. The islands have been inhabited since prehistoric times, and their strategic location in the Mediterranean has made them a focal point for various civilizations. From the ancient Phoenicians and Romans to the Knights of St. John and the British Empire, Malta has absorbed influences from diverse cultures, which is reflected in its architecture, language, and traditions. As you explore, you will encounter megalithic temples that date back thousands of years, charming fishing villages, and bustling towns that showcase the rich tapestry of Maltese life.

Malta's culture is another aspect that sets it apart. The islands boast a lively arts scene, with numerous festivals, concerts, and exhibitions happening throughout the year. Traditional Maltese cuisine is also a highlight, offering a delightful blend of Mediterranean flavors. Be sure to try local dishes such as pastizzi, rabbit stew, and fresh seafood, which reflect the island's culinary heritage.

Getting around Malta is relatively easy, with a well-connected public transport system that allows you to explore both the bustling cities and serene countryside. Whether you choose to take a bus, rent a car, or even hop on a ferry, the choice is yours. This flexibility gives you the opportunity to tailor your experience and discover the islands at your own pace.

As you read through this guide, you will find detailed information on top attractions, scenic itineraries, hidden gems, and local insights that will enhance your experience in Malta. From historical sites to breathtaking natural wonders, from vibrant nightlife to peaceful retreats, Malta offers a diverse range of experiences that cater to all interests and preferences.

This guide is here to help you make the most of your visit, providing you with the tools to create unforgettable memories. So, whether you are looking to immerse yourself in history, relax on a sun-kissed beach, or savor delicious local food, Malta is a destination that promises to exceed your expectations. We invite you to turn the pages and embark on your adventure through this captivating archipelago, where every corner has a story to tell and every moment is an opportunity to create lasting memories.

CHAPTER 1

DISCOVERING MALTA

The History of Malta

The history of Malta is a rich tapestry woven from centuries of diverse influences, cultures, and events. This small archipelago, situated in the heart of the Mediterranean Sea, has been inhabited since prehistoric times and has witnessed the rise and fall of various civilizations, each leaving its mark on the islands. Understanding Malta's history requires an appreciation of its geographical significance, as its location has made it a crossroads for trade and military conquests throughout the ages.

The earliest evidence of human settlement in Malta dates back to around 5200 BC, when Neolithic people arrived from nearby Sicily. These early settlers were skilled farmers and craftsmen who built impressive megalithic temples, some of which are still standing today, like the temples of Ħaġar Qim and Mnajdra. These ancient structures are among the oldest free-standing buildings in the world, and they reflect the advanced architectural knowledge of these early inhabitants. The temples were used for religious purposes and demonstrate a deep connection to the spiritual beliefs of the people who lived here thousands of years ago.

Around 2500 BC, the island saw the arrival of the Bronze Age, which brought new influences from neighboring cultures. During this time, the Maltese people developed new tools and pottery styles, and trade with other civilizations began to flourish. This period was followed by the Phoenicians, who arrived around 800 BC. The Phoenicians were skilled traders and seafarers, and they established Malta as a key trading post. They contributed to the development of local industry and introduced the art of writing, which had a profound impact on the islands.

Following the Phoenicians, the islands came under the rule of the Carthaginians around 600 BC. The Carthaginians expanded trade and agriculture and strengthened Malta's position as a commercial hub in the Mediterranean. However, their influence was short-lived, as the Romans began their conquest of the Mediterranean in the 3rd century BC. By 218 BC, Malta had become part of the Roman Empire. Under Roman rule, Malta enjoyed a period of relative peace and prosperity. The Romans built roads, temples, and public buildings, and the islands flourished as a center of trade. The Roman period also saw the spread of Christianity, which would play a significant role in Malta's future.

In 476 AD, the Western Roman Empire fell, and Malta became part of the Byzantine Empire. During this time, the islands faced challenges from invading tribes and piracy, which disrupted trade. The Byzantines fortified the islands to protect against these threats and maintained their Christian presence. However, in the 9th century, the Arabs invaded Malta, marking a new chapter in its history. The Arab influence introduced new agricultural practices, such as irrigation, and the cultivation of crops like citrus fruits and sugar cane. They also contributed to the development of the Maltese language, which still contains many Arabic words today.

In 1091, the Normans conquered Malta, and the islands became part of the Kingdom of Sicily. The Normans established a feudal system and promoted the spread of Christianity. This period also marked the beginning of a long-standing connection between Malta and the Knights of St. John, who would later play a crucial role in the islands' history. In 1530, Holy Roman Emperor Charles V granted the islands to the Knights, who sought refuge from the Ottoman Empire. The Knights fortified the islands, constructed magnificent buildings, and turned Valletta into a stronghold.

The most significant event in Malta's history occurred in 1565 when the Ottomans launched a massive invasion to capture the islands. The Great Siege of Malta saw the Knights, along with the local population, bravely defending the islands against overwhelming odds. After several months of intense fighting, the Knights emerged victorious, and this victory solidified Malta's reputation as a key player in Mediterranean politics. The victory during the siege allowed the Knights to further develop the islands, leading to the construction of the impressive city of Valletta, named after Grand Master Jean Parisot de la Valette.

The following centuries were marked by the Knights' rule, which continued until 1798 when Napoleon Bonaparte captured Malta during his campaign in the Mediterranean. Although the French occupation was short-lived, it brought significant changes, including the introduction of new laws and administrative systems. In 1800, the British, who were concerned about French expansion, took control of Malta. The British period lasted for over a century and saw the modernization of the islands' infrastructure, education, and economy. Malta played a vital role during both World Wars, serving as a strategic base for the Allies in the Mediterranean.

Following World War II, Malta began to push for independence. In 1964, Malta gained independence from British rule, becoming a republic in 1974. The islands continued to develop as a nation, embracing their rich history and cultural heritage while also modernizing their economy. In 2004, Malta joined the European Union, which further integrated the islands into the global community.

Today, Malta is known for its vibrant culture, stunning architecture, and historical significance. The influences of the various civilizations that have occupied the islands can be seen in everything from the local cuisine to the languages spoken. The blend of cultures creates a unique atmosphere that attracts visitors from around the world. As you explore Malta, you will encounter ancient ruins, medieval fortifications, and charming villages that tell the story of its past. The islands continue to thrive as a popular tourist destination, offering a rich tapestry of experiences for those who seek to understand the history and culture of this remarkable archipelago.

The Maltese Culture and Traditions

The culture and traditions of Malta are a vibrant mix of influences from various civilizations that have inhabited the islands over the centuries. This small archipelago, located in the central Mediterranean, has a rich history that has shaped its unique identity. The Maltese people take great pride in their heritage, which is reflected in their language, customs, and daily life.

One of the most distinctive aspects of Maltese culture is the Maltese language, which is a blend of Arabic, Italian, and English influences. Maltese is the only official language of Arabic descent in the European Union. The language has its roots in the Arabic spoken by the Arab rulers who occupied the islands from the 9th to the 11th centuries. Over the years, it has evolved and incorporated many Italian and English words, making it a truly unique language that reflects the islands' diverse history. Maltese is used in everyday conversations, as well as in literature and media, and it plays an essential role in maintaining the cultural identity of the people.

Religious traditions hold a central place in Maltese culture, with the majority of the population identifying as Roman Catholic. The church has historically influenced many aspects of daily life and continues to play a significant role in the community. The Maltese are known for their strong sense of faith, which is often expressed through elaborate church feasts and celebrations. These feasts, known as "festa," occur throughout the year in different villages, celebrating the patron saints of each locality. The festas are marked by vibrant processions, fireworks, and music, creating a festive atmosphere that brings the community together. People dress in traditional clothing, and the streets are adorned with colorful decorations, showcasing the deep-rooted religious devotion and local pride.

Cuisine is another essential element of Maltese culture, heavily influenced by Mediterranean flavors and ingredients. Traditional dishes often feature fresh seafood, locally grown vegetables, and a variety of herbs and spices. One of the most famous dishes is "fenek," or rabbit stew, which is considered the national dish of Malta. It is typically slow-cooked with garlic, wine, and spices, resulting in a flavorful meal that reflects the islands' culinary traditions. Other popular dishes include "pastizzi," flaky pastries filled with ricotta cheese or peas, and "bragioli," beef olives filled with minced meat and herbs. The food culture also emphasizes communal dining, where families and friends gather to enjoy meals together, reinforcing social bonds and a sense of community.

Music and dance are integral to Maltese culture, with a rich tradition of folk music that has been passed down through generations. Traditional Maltese music often features instruments like the "għana," a type of sung poetry, and the "zucchini," a local string instrument. Folk songs often tell stories of love, life, and the islands' history. During village festas, music fills the air, with bands playing lively tunes that invite people to dance and celebrate together. Dance is often spontaneous, with people joining in as they feel the rhythm, creating a sense of joy and unity among participants.

Art also plays a vital role in Maltese culture, with a history that dates back to prehistoric times. The temples built by ancient civilizations are not only architectural marvels but also artistic expressions of the time. In more recent history, the Knights of St. John left their mark through baroque architecture, particularly in Valletta, where stunning churches and palaces showcase intricate designs and craftsmanship. Today, contemporary Maltese artists continue to contribute to the cultural landscape, exploring themes that reflect both local and global influences. Art exhibitions and galleries can be found throughout the islands, highlighting the work of both established and emerging artists.

Another significant aspect of Maltese culture is its strong sense of community and family ties. Maltese people often prioritize family above all else, and it is common for extended families to live close together. This closeness fosters a supportive environment where family gatherings are frequent, and traditions are shared from one generation to the next. Celebrations such as weddings and christenings are grand affairs, filled with rituals and customs that reflect the community's values and beliefs. It is not uncommon for these events to be large and extravagant, showcasing the importance of social connections and cultural identity.

Sports also hold a special place in Maltese culture, with football being the most popular sport on the islands. The national football team has a dedicated following, and local clubs play a significant role in fostering community spirit. Other sports, such as water polo and rugby, are also enjoyed, and the beautiful Mediterranean waters provide ample opportunities for sailing, diving, and other water sports. Sporting events often bring communities together, allowing people to cheer for their teams and celebrate their achievements.

The influence of tourism on Maltese culture cannot be understated. With millions of visitors flocking to the islands each year, the local culture is both enriched and challenged by the influx of different perspectives and practices. Tourism has led to a greater appreciation for local traditions, with many initiatives aimed at preserving cultural heritage.

Visitors are often eager to engage with the local community, whether through culinary experiences, workshops, or guided tours that highlight traditional crafts and practices. This exchange fosters a greater understanding and appreciation of Maltese culture, allowing for a unique blending of old and new.

As Malta continues to evolve, its culture remains deeply rooted in history while adapting to modern influences. The Maltese people proudly embrace their heritage, sharing it with visitors who come to experience the islands' rich traditions and vibrant way of life. From language and cuisine to music and art, every aspect of Maltese culture tells a story of resilience, unity, and a deep connection to the land and its history. As you explore Malta, you will not only witness the beauty of its landscapes but also the warmth of its people and the richness of its traditions, making your journey truly unforgettable.

The Best Time to Visit Malta

Deciding when to visit Malta involves understanding the unique climate, events, and experiences that each season offers. Malta has a Mediterranean climate, characterized by hot, dry summers and mild, wet winters. This climate makes it a year-round destination, but certain times of the year can enhance your experience, depending on your preferences for activities, weather, and crowd levels.

The peak tourist season in Malta runs from June to September, when the weather is at its hottest and sunniest. During these months, visitors can expect daytime temperatures to reach well into the 30s Celsius (mid-80s to mid-90s Fahrenheit). This is the ideal time for beach lovers who want to enjoy the islands' beautiful coastlines, crystal-clear waters, and warm sunshine. The beaches are lively, with sunbathers and swimmers taking full advantage of the summer heat. Many water sports are available, such as snorkeling, diving, and sailing. Furthermore, numerous outdoor festivals and events take place during the summer, allowing visitors to experience local culture through food, music, and traditional celebrations.

However, while the summer months are perfect for sun-seekers, they can also bring large crowds and higher prices for accommodations and activities. Major tourist spots can feel crowded, and the vibrant nightlife scene means that some areas might be noisier than usual. If you prefer a more laid-back atmosphere, it might be wise to consider visiting during the shoulder seasons of spring and fall.

Spring, particularly April to May, is a fantastic time to visit Malta. During these months, the weather is pleasantly warm, with temperatures ranging from 18 to 27 degrees Celsius (64 to 81 degrees Fahrenheit). This is an ideal time for outdoor activities such as hiking, exploring historical sites, and taking part in local events without the intense heat of summer. The landscape comes alive with blooming flowers, and the countryside is lush and green after the winter rains. This season also marks the beginning of many local festivals, including Easter celebrations, which feature colorful processions and traditional events. Visiting during spring allows you to enjoy the beauty of the islands while avoiding the summer rush.

Autumn, particularly September to October, is another excellent time to experience Malta. The weather remains warm, with temperatures ranging from 20 to 30 degrees Celsius (68 to 86 degrees Fahrenheit), and the sea is still warm enough for swimming. This season also marks the end of the peak tourist season, which means that crowds begin to thin out, making it easier to explore popular attractions. Many local festivals and events occur during this time, including the famous Notte Bianca in October, which features art, music, and culture across Valletta. Autumn is also a great time for food lovers, as the harvest season brings fresh produce, and many restaurants showcase local ingredients in their dishes.

If you are looking for a quieter experience, winter months from November to March offer a completely different side of Malta. While temperatures can drop to around 10 to 20 degrees Celsius (50 to 68 degrees Fahrenheit), this period is characterized by mild weather and occasional rainfall. Winter is the best time to explore the islands' rich history and culture without the crowds. The streets of Valletta and Mdina are less busy, allowing for a more relaxed exploration of historical sites, museums, and churches. The holiday season also brings festive decorations and local traditions, especially during Christmas and New Year's. You can experience local markets, concerts, and unique cultural celebrations that give a different flavor to the Maltese experience.

Another consideration when planning your visit is the variety of events that take place throughout the year. Malta hosts a range of cultural festivals, concerts, and exhibitions, many of which are tied to the local calendar. For instance, the Malta International Arts Festival, held in summer, features a mix of music, dance, and visual arts, attracting both local and international talent. The Carnival in February is another vibrant event, with colorful parades and celebrations that showcase Maltese traditions. Understanding the event calendar can help you plan your visit to coincide with activities that interest you.

The best time to visit Malta depends on your preferences and what you want to experience. If you enjoy warm weather and lively beaches, the summer months will suit you. If you prefer milder temperatures and fewer crowds, consider visiting in the spring or fall. Those seeking a quieter, more cultural experience might find winter to be the most rewarding time to explore the islands. Regardless of when you choose to visit, Malta's rich history, stunning landscapes, and warm hospitality are sure to make your trip memorable.

CHAPTER 2

PRACTICAL INFORMATION

Accommodations: Where to Stay

Luxury Accommodation Options

For travelers looking to experience the finest in luxury while visiting Malta, the island offers a range of high-end accommodation options that combine elegance, comfort, and impeccable service. These luxury hotels and resorts cater to those who want to indulge in the best that Malta has to offer, providing not just a place to stay but an experience that enhances your visit. Each of these accommodations offers unique features, from stunning sea views and world-class spas to gourmet dining and exclusive amenities. Whether you're celebrating a special occasion, planning a romantic getaway, or simply looking to enjoy the highest standard of comfort and service, these luxury options provide the perfect base for your Maltese adventure.

One of the most highly recommended luxury accommodations is The Phoenicia Malta, a five-star hotel located right at the entrance of Valletta. With its historic charm, elegant decor, and prime location, The Phoenicia is often considered one of Malta's best hotels. It offers a variety of rooms and suites, each beautifully furnished with a blend of classic and contemporary styles. The hotel's lush gardens, outdoor pool overlooking the harbor, and stunning views of Valletta's skyline create a tranquil and luxurious setting. Prices for a standard room range from around €250 to €400 per night, depending on the season, while suites can go up to €1,200 or more. The hotel also features fine dining options, a chic bar, and a wellness center, making it ideal for those looking to unwind in style. To get to The Phoenicia from Malta International Airport, you can take a taxi, which takes approximately 20 minutes, or opt for a private car service arranged through the hotel. Booking can be done directly on their website or through luxury hotel platforms like Booking.com or Expedia, ensuring you find the best rates and exclusive offers.

Another top choice for luxury accommodation is The Westin Dragonara Resort, located in the lively area of St. Julian's. This five-star resort is known for its spacious rooms, spectacular sea views, and private beach area, making it a favorite for both couples and families. The Westin Dragonara offers a range of amenities, including multiple swimming pools, a full-service spa, a fitness center, and several on-site restaurants that serve everything from Mediterranean cuisine to fresh seafood. Rooms typically start at around €200 per night, while premium suites can go up to €600 or more, offering extra space and upgraded features like private terraces. The resort's location in St. Julian's makes it convenient for exploring the area's vibrant nightlife, dining, and shopping options. To reach the Westin

Dragonara from the airport, you can take a taxi, which takes about 25 minutes, or use the hotel's private transfer service. Booking can be done through the hotel's official website, or you can find exclusive deals and packages on platforms like Marriott's Bonvoy or other high-end booking sites.

For those seeking a more secluded and intimate experience, The Xara Palace Relais & Châteaux in Mdina is an excellent option. This boutique hotel, set in a 17th-century palace, is located within the ancient walls of Malta's "Silent City." With only 17 individually designed rooms and suites, The Xara Palace offers a unique blend of history, luxury, and personalized service. Each room is decorated with antique furnishings, original artwork, and offers views of the Maltese countryside or the historic city of Mdina. Prices range from €300 to €800 per night, depending on the room category and season. The Xara Palace is known for its fine dining restaurant, de Mondion, which has earned a reputation as one of Malta's best restaurants. The hotel also offers private tours and experiences for guests, making it perfect for those looking to immerse themselves in the island's history and culture. To get to The Xara Palace from the airport, you can take a taxi, which takes about 30 minutes, or arrange a private transfer through the hotel. Booking can be made directly through the hotel's website or through the Relais & Châteaux network for additional perks.

For a luxurious seaside retreat, consider Kempinski Hotel San Lawrenz on the island of Gozo. This five-star resort is surrounded by lush gardens and offers a peaceful escape from the hustle and bustle of Malta's main island. The Kempinski is known for its spacious rooms, traditional Gozitan architecture, and a focus on wellness. It features a large spa offering a variety of treatments, indoor and outdoor pools, and gourmet dining options that highlight local ingredients. Room rates start at around €150 per night, while suites and family rooms can go up to €500, making it a great choice for both couples and families. The resort's rural location provides easy access to some of Gozo's top attractions, such as the Azure Window, the Ggantija Temples, and the beautiful beaches of Ramla Bay. To reach the Kempinski from Malta International Airport, you'll need to take a taxi to the Cirkewwa Ferry Terminal (about 45 minutes), then take the Gozo ferry to Mgarr, and finally a short 15-minute drive to the hotel. Booking is available through the Kempinski website or luxury travel platforms like Leading Hotels of the World.

Finally, for those seeking the ultimate luxury experience, Corinthia Palace Hotel & Spa in Attard is a top contender. This elegant five-star hotel is set in a beautifully restored 19th-century villa and is known for its refined atmosphere, excellent service, and focus on wellness. The hotel offers a range of luxurious rooms and suites, each decorated in a classic style with modern touches. Prices for a standard room start at around €250 per night, while suites can go up to €700 or more, depending on the season and availability. The Corinthia Palace features an award-winning spa, outdoor and indoor pools, and a range of dining options, including a fine-dining restaurant and a more casual brasserie. The hotel's location in the quiet village of Attard makes it an ideal base for exploring central Malta, including the nearby San Anton Gardens and the historic town of Mdina. To get to the Corinthia Palace from the airport, a taxi ride takes about 20 minutes, or you can arrange a private transfer through the hotel. Booking can be made on the Corinthia website or through other luxury hotel platforms for exclusive packages and discounts.

Each of these luxury accommodations offers something unique, whether it's a historic setting, a focus on wellness, or stunning seaside views. By choosing one of these high-end options, you'll not only have a comfortable place to stay but also a memorable experience that adds to the enjoyment of your trip. To ensure you get the best rates and availability, it's always a good idea to book early and consider any special offers or packages that might enhance your stay. Whether you're looking for a romantic escape, a family-friendly resort, or a tranquil retreat, these luxury accommodations in Malta provide the perfect base for an unforgettable vacation.

Budget Options

For travelers visiting Malta on a budget, there are many affordable accommodation options that still provide comfort, convenience, and a good location without breaking the bank. Malta's budget-friendly accommodations range from small guesthouses and charming boutique hostels to family-run hotels that offer great value for money. Whether you're a backpacker, a solo traveler, or a family looking for a reasonably priced place to stay, this guide will highlight some of the best budget accommodations in Malta, along with their price range, amenities, and tips on how to reach them from the main airports. Choosing a budget accommodation doesn't mean compromising on quality or experience; in fact, many of these options provide unique atmospheres, friendly service, and the chance to stay in some of the island's most interesting areas.

One popular budget option is Marco Polo Hostel in St. Julian's, a lively town known for its nightlife and close proximity to some of Malta's best beaches. Marco Polo Hostel is ideal for young travelers and those looking to meet others, as it has a vibrant social atmosphere and offers a variety of dormitory rooms as well as private rooms. Dormitory beds start at around €15 per night, while private rooms can range from €40 to €70 per night, making it one of the most affordable options in the area. The hostel features a spacious rooftop terrace with a bar and views of the town, shared kitchen facilities, a TV lounge, and free Wi-Fi throughout the property. Located in the heart of St. Julian's, Marco Polo Hostel is just a short walk from Paceville's nightlife district and the sandy beach at St. George's Bay. To get there from Malta International Airport, you can take a direct taxi, which takes about 20 minutes, or use public transportation by taking Bus X2 to St. Julian's. Booking can be done directly on the hostel's website or through popular budget platforms like Hostelworld, ensuring you find the best rates and availability.

Another great option for budget-conscious travelers is Two Pillows Boutique Hostel in Sliema, a bustling town just across the harbor from Valletta. Two Pillows is a stylish and comfortable hostel that offers both dormitory beds and private rooms, catering to a range of budgets. Prices for a dormitory bed start at around €25 per night, while private rooms range from €50 to €100, depending on the room type and season. The hostel is set in a restored townhouse and has a welcoming atmosphere, with features like a rooftop terrace, a fully equipped kitchen, and even a small wellness area with a sauna and Jacuzzi. It's a great place for travelers looking for a bit more comfort and privacy while staying within a budget. Sliema's central location makes it easy to explore the rest of Malta, with ferries to Valletta just a few minutes away and plenty of shops, cafés, and restaurants nearby. To reach Two Pillows from the airport, take Bus X2 to Sliema, which takes about 30 minutes, or opt for a taxi, which takes around 20 minutes. Booking can be made through the hostel's website or on platforms like Booking.com, where you can read reviews and compare prices.

For those seeking a quieter, more local experience, Rokon Apartments in Mellieha is an excellent choice. Mellieha is a charming village in the northern part of Malta, known for its stunning sandy beaches and laid-back atmosphere. Rokon Apartments offer self-catering studios and one-bedroom apartments, making them ideal for budget travelers who prefer to have their own space and cook some of their own meals. Prices start at around €40 per night for a studio and €60 for a one-bedroom apartment, depending on the season. The apartments are simply furnished but clean and well-maintained, with kitchenettes, private bathrooms, and balconies overlooking the village or the countryside. The location is perfect for beach lovers, as Mellieha Bay, one of Malta's largest sandy beaches, is just a short walk away. To reach Rokon Apartments from the airport, you can take Bus X1 directly to Mellieha, which takes about an hour, or a taxi, which takes around 45 minutes. Booking can be done through Airbnb or the apartment's direct website, where you may also find longer-stay discounts.

For a unique stay with a focus on community and eco-conscious living, consider The Splendid Guesthouse in Mellieha. This family-run guesthouse offers a friendly atmosphere and a welcoming environment at very affordable prices. Rooms start at around €45 per night, including breakfast, making it a great deal for budget travelers. The Splendid Guesthouse features a rooftop terrace, a shared kitchen, and a comfortable lounge area where guests can relax and mingle. The owners are known for their warm hospitality and are happy to provide recommendations for exploring the local area. Mellieha's location makes it a great base for exploring both the northern coast of Malta and the nearby island of Gozo, which is accessible via a short ferry ride. To reach The Splendid Guesthouse, take Bus X1 from the airport to Mellieha, or opt for a taxi for a quicker, more direct route. Booking can be made through the guesthouse's website or platforms like Agoda, where you can find exclusive deals.

Lastly, for travelers who prefer a hostel with a bit more privacy and tranquility, Inhawi Boutique Hostel in St. Julian's offers a budget-friendly yet stylish stay. Inhawi is located on a quiet street near Balluta Bay, providing easy access to the beach and local restaurants. The hostel has both dormitory and private rooms, with dorm beds starting at around €20 per night and private rooms ranging from €60 to €120, depending on the season. The hostel features a beautiful garden with a pool, a shared kitchen, and a terrace with sea views. It's perfect for those who want to enjoy a more relaxed atmosphere while still being close to the action. To reach Inhawi Boutique Hostel from the airport, take Bus X2 to St. Julian's, which takes around 30 minutes, or a taxi, which takes about 20 minutes. Booking can be made through the hostel's website or on Hostelworld, where you can read reviews and find the best deals.

Each of these budget options offers something unique, whether it's a social atmosphere, the chance to cook your own meals, or a quiet retreat away from the more touristy areas. By choosing one of these accommodations, you'll be able to enjoy a comfortable stay in Malta without overspending, freeing up more of your budget for exploring the island's attractions, dining out, and enjoying all that Malta has to offer. Booking early is recommended, as budget accommodations tend to fill up quickly, especially during the high season. Look for special offers and discounts on platforms like Booking.com, Hostelworld, or directly on the properties' websites to get the best value for your stay. With the right planning, you can have an enjoyable and affordable trip to Malta, experiencing the island's beauty and culture while staying within your budget.

Unique Accommodation Options

For travelers seeking an extraordinary stay in Malta, there are a variety of unique accommodation options that go beyond the typical hotels and resorts. These special places offer a chance to experience the island in a different light, combining distinct settings, historical charm, and personalized touches to make your visit truly memorable. From charming boutique guesthouses to restored palazzos and countryside farmhouses, each of these accommodations provides a unique atmosphere that captures the essence of Malta's heritage and natural beauty. This guide will highlight some of the most remarkable places to stay, providing detailed information on price ranges, amenities, and how to reach them from the airport. These options are ideal for those looking to add a touch of individuality and character to their trip, ensuring a stay that is as unique as the island itself.

One standout choice for a unique stay is Locanda La Gelsomina, a boutique guesthouse located in the historic town of Birgu (Vittoriosa), one of Malta's oldest settlements. Set in a 16th-century building, this beautifully restored guesthouse offers a blend of authentic Maltese architecture and Asian-inspired decor, creating a tranquil and luxurious atmosphere. Each of the four suites is uniquely designed, featuring antique furnishings, fine textiles, and modern amenities such as air conditioning, free Wi-Fi, and a private balcony or terrace. The price per night starts at around €180 for a standard suite and can go up to €350 for the larger suites, depending on the season. Guests can enjoy a delicious breakfast in the serene courtyard, which is filled with lush plants and the scent of jasmine. The guesthouse's central location in Birgu makes it easy to explore the Three Cities and the Grand Harbour area. To reach Locanda La Gelsomina from Malta International Airport, you can take a taxi, which takes about 20 minutes, or use public transportation by taking Bus X4 to Valletta, followed by a ferry across the harbor to Birgu. Booking is available through their official website or luxury travel platforms like Mr & Mrs Smith.

Another option that offers a unique blend of history and comfort is Casa Ellul, a boutique hotel in Valletta. Housed in a 19th-century palazzo, Casa Ellul has been meticulously restored to preserve its historical features while incorporating modern design elements. Each of the nine suites is individually styled, with original tiled floors, high ceilings, and views of Valletta's historic skyline. The atmosphere is intimate and sophisticated, making it perfect for couples looking for a romantic retreat. Prices start at around €200 per night for a standard suite and can reach up to €450 for the penthouse suite, which features a private rooftop terrace with a hot tub. Guests can enjoy a continental breakfast in the hotel's cozy dining room or order room service for a more private experience. The central location allows easy access to Valletta's main attractions, including St. John's Co-Cathedral, the Upper Barrakka Gardens, and the bustling Strait Street. To get to Casa Ellul from the airport, a taxi ride takes about 15 minutes, or you can take Bus X4 or X5 directly to Valletta. Booking can be done through their website or on popular platforms like Small Luxury Hotels.

For those looking to escape the hustle and bustle of the main island, Ta' Cenc Hotel & Spa on Gozo offers a unique retreat surrounded by nature. Located on a 400-acre estate in the village of Sannat, this eco-friendly hotel blends into the Gozitan landscape with its stone-built bungalows and suites. The hotel is known for its stunning views of the Mediterranean Sea, tranquil setting, and emphasis on relaxation and wellness. Prices for a standard room start at around €140 per night, while suites and family rooms can go up to €300 or more. Ta' Cenc features a full-service spa, outdoor and indoor pools, tennis courts, and several dining options that serve fresh local ingredients. The property's extensive grounds are ideal for leisurely walks, and the nearby Ta' Cenc Cliffs offer some of the best hiking and birdwatching opportunities in Gozo. To reach Ta' Cenc from Malta International Airport, take a taxi to Cirkewwa Ferry Terminal (about 45 minutes), then take the ferry to Mgarr, and a short 20-minute drive from the Gozo ferry port to the hotel. Booking can be made through the hotel's website or on eco-friendly travel platforms that specialize in sustainable stays.

If you're looking for a place with deep historical roots, Palazzo Prince d'Orange in Valletta is a fantastic option. This elegant property dates back to the 17th century and was once home to the Knights of St. John. Today, it has been transformed into a boutique residence offering five luxurious suites that combine classic charm with modern comforts. The suites feature high ceilings, original wooden beams, and views of the Grand Harbour or Valletta's quaint streets. Prices start at around €150 per night for a one-bedroom suite and can go up to €300 for the larger, two-bedroom suites. Guests have access to a shared rooftop terrace, a lounge, and a small fitness area. Palazzo Prince d'Orange's location in the heart of Valletta makes it perfect for those who want to explore the city's rich history and cultural attractions. To reach the palazzo from the airport, a taxi takes about 15 minutes, or you can use public transport by taking Bus X4 to Valletta. Booking can be arranged through their website or high-end travel platforms like Airbnb Luxe.

For a truly unique experience that combines traditional Maltese countryside living with modern luxury, consider staying at Lulu Boutique Hotel in Zebbug. This charming guesthouse is set in a traditional Maltese townhouse, featuring a beautiful courtyard, a rooftop terrace, and tastefully decorated rooms that reflect the building's heritage. Prices start at around €80 per night for a standard room and go up to €180 for the larger suites. The hotel's central location in the village of Zebbug provides a quiet and authentic experience, away from the main tourist areas. Guests can relax in the peaceful courtyard, enjoy a homemade breakfast, and explore the nearby countryside. The rooftop terrace offers stunning views of the village and surrounding hills, making it an ideal spot for sunset drinks. To reach Lulu Boutique Hotel from the airport, a taxi takes around 25 minutes, or you can take Bus X3 to Zebbug. Booking is available through their website or boutique hotel platforms like i-escape.

Each of these unique accommodation options provides more than just a place to stay—they offer an experience that adds to your overall enjoyment of Malta. Whether you're looking for historic charm, a peaceful retreat, or a stylish boutique stay, these properties cater to different tastes and preferences while maintaining a high standard of service and comfort. By choosing one of these unique accommodations, you'll be able to create a more personal and memorable experience during your visit to Malta. To secure your preferred dates and ensure availability, it's best to book early, especially during peak travel seasons. Use a combination of direct booking and trusted travel platforms to find the best deals and any special packages that might enhance your stay.

Best Areas to Stay in Malta

Choosing where to stay in Malta depends on what kind of experience you want to have during your visit. Each area of Malta has its own unique character, attractions, and atmosphere, making it important to select the right location that aligns with your interests. From bustling cities and lively coastal towns to quieter villages and picturesque countryside settings, Malta offers a variety of accommodations and surroundings that cater to different preferences.

One of the most popular areas to stay in is Valletta, the capital city of Malta. This historic city is a UNESCO World Heritage site and is known for its stunning architecture, beautiful harbors, and rich cultural heritage. Staying in Valletta is ideal for those who want to be in the heart of Malta's history and culture. You'll find numerous museums, churches, and palaces, as well as lively cafes and restaurants. The city is very compact, so it's easy to walk around and explore. Because it is centrally located, Valletta is also well-connected to other parts of the island, making it a convenient base for day trips. Accommodations here range from luxury hotels housed in historic buildings to charming boutique guesthouses that offer a more intimate experience.

Another great place to stay is Sliema, which is situated just across the harbor from Valletta. Sliema is known for its modern vibe and offers a mix of shopping, dining, and nightlife options. It has a lively seafront promenade, lined with cafes and bars, making it a popular spot for evening strolls. This area is perfect for those who want to be close to Valletta but prefer a more contemporary setting. Sliema also has a range of accommodations, from upscale hotels to budget-friendly options, and many of them offer stunning sea views. It is also a hub for ferries and boat tours, providing easy access to explore other parts of the island by sea.

For travelers seeking a livelier atmosphere, St. Julian's is a top choice. Located just north of Sliema, St. Julian's is famous for its nightlife, entertainment, and dining options. The neighborhood of Paceville, in particular, is known for its clubs, bars, and casinos, attracting younger travelers and those looking for a vibrant nightlife scene. However, St. Julian's is not just about partying—it also has beautiful coastal areas, such as Spinola Bay, which is lined with traditional Maltese boats and seafood restaurants. St. George's Bay, a small sandy beach, is also in this area and is a nice spot for a swim. Accommodations in St. Julian's range from large international hotels to stylish apartments, making it a good option for all types of travelers.

If you prefer a more relaxed and picturesque setting, the area of Mellieħa in the northern part of Malta is a wonderful option. Mellieħa is known for its stunning sandy beaches, clear waters, and scenic views. It is home to Mellieħa Bay, the largest sandy beach in Malta, which is ideal for families and beach lovers. The area has a more tranquil vibe compared to the busier southern parts of the island, making it perfect for those who want to unwind and enjoy the natural beauty of Malta. Mellieħa also offers access to some of the best hiking trails, such as those that lead to the secluded Paradise Bay. Accommodations here include beach resorts, boutique hotels, and family-friendly apartments.

For those interested in a more traditional experience, staying in the ancient city of Mdina is highly recommended. Mdina is known as the "Silent City" because of its quiet, traffic-free streets. This small walled city, with its medieval and baroque architecture, transports visitors back in time. Staying in Mdina is ideal for history enthusiasts and those looking for a peaceful retreat. The accommodations here are limited and often include historic palazzos converted into elegant guesthouses, offering a truly unique experience. Although Mdina is small, it is well-positioned for exploring the rest of Malta, and its proximity to Rabat adds more options for dining and sightseeing.

Another interesting area to consider is the Three Cities, which consists of Birgu (Vittoriosa), Senglea, and Cospicua. These cities are older than Valletta and offer a glimpse into Malta's maritime history. The Three Cities are less crowded and more residential, providing an authentic local experience. Staying here allows visitors to explore narrow streets, traditional Maltese houses, and picturesque marinas. The area has a range of accommodations, from budget options to luxurious boutique hotels overlooking the Grand Harbour. The Three Cities are also well-connected to Valletta by ferry, making it easy to access the capital while enjoying a quieter base.

If you're planning to explore Malta's sister island, Gozo, you might want to consider staying in Victoria, the capital of Gozo. Victoria, also known as Rabat, is the cultural and commercial heart of the island. The Cittadella, a historic fortified city, sits atop the town and offers panoramic views of the entire island. Staying in Victoria is convenient for those who want to explore Gozo's attractions, such as the Ggantija Temples and the picturesque coastal village of Xlendi. Gozo is quieter and more rural than the main island of Malta, making it ideal for those seeking a slower pace and a more nature-focused experience. Accommodations in Gozo range from traditional farmhouses to modern hotels, providing a variety of options.

Another beautiful area on Gozo is the village of Marsalforn, which is popular for its beaches and relaxed seaside atmosphere. Marsalforn is a great base for exploring Gozo's northern coast and is known for its diving spots and seafood restaurants. It has a more laid-back vibe, making it suitable for those who want to enjoy a peaceful stay by the sea.

In addition to these main areas, there are many other smaller towns and villages across Malta that offer unique experiences and accommodations. Places like Marsaxlokk, a traditional fishing village in the southeast, are perfect for those looking for a more authentic, local experience. Here, visitors can enjoy fresh seafood, explore local markets, and watch the colorful fishing boats bobbing in the harbor. The accommodations are typically smaller guesthouses or family-run bed and breakfasts, providing a cozy and personal touch.

The best area to stay in Malta depends on your preferences, whether you're looking for a lively atmosphere, historical charm, or a peaceful beachside retreat. Each area has its own appeal and offers a different perspective on life in Malta, making it important to choose a location that matches what you want to experience during your visit. No matter where you decide to stay, you'll find that Malta's small size makes it easy to explore all its corners, ensuring that you get the most out of your time on these beautiful islands.

Recommended Hotels and Hostels

When visiting Malta, choosing the right place to stay is crucial to ensuring a comfortable and enjoyable experience. The island offers a wide range of accommodations, from luxury hotels to budget-friendly hostels, catering to different preferences and budgets. Here are some recommended hotels and hostels, including their price ranges, amenities, and how to find them, as well as information on getting there from the major airports.

One highly recommended hotel is the InterContinental Malta, located in St. Julian's. This five-star hotel offers luxurious accommodations with stunning views of the Mediterranean Sea. The rooms are spacious and elegantly decorated, featuring modern amenities such as free Wi-Fi, flat-screen TVs, and minibars. Guests can enjoy multiple on-site restaurants serving a variety of cuisines, a large outdoor pool, and a well-equipped fitness center. The hotel also has a spa for relaxation and wellness treatments. Prices typically range from €150 to €300 per night, depending on the season and room type. To reach the InterContinental Malta from Malta International Airport, you can take a taxi, which takes about 20 minutes, or use public transport, which involves taking a bus to St. Julian's and then walking to the hotel. Booking can be done through the hotel's official website, major travel booking sites, or by contacting the hotel directly.

Another excellent option is the Palazzo Consiglia, a boutique hotel located in Valletta. This hotel is known for its blend of modern luxury and historic charm, set within a beautifully restored 17th-century building. Rooms are tastefully furnished and come equipped with free Wi-Fi, air conditioning, and coffee-making facilities. The hotel offers a rooftop pool, a fitness center, and a complimentary breakfast. Prices generally range from €100 to €250 per night. The Palazzo Consiglia is easily accessible from Malta International Airport via taxi, taking around 20 minutes, or by bus to Valletta followed by a short walk. Reservations can be made through the hotel's website or popular travel booking platforms.

For travelers looking for a more budget-friendly option, The British Hotel in Valletta offers affordable yet comfortable accommodations. This family-run hotel provides basic amenities, including free Wi-Fi, air conditioning, and a restaurant with a terrace overlooking the Grand Harbour. The rooms are simple but clean, making it a great choice for those who want to explore the city without breaking the bank. Prices range from €50 to €120 per night, depending on the season. The British Hotel is conveniently located within walking distance of many historical sites and attractions. To reach the hotel from Malta International Airport, you can take a taxi for about 20 minutes or use the bus service to Valletta. Booking can be done directly through the hotel's website or through various online travel agencies.

Another great accommodation option is Sliema Marina Hotel, situated in Sliema along the seafront. This three-star hotel offers a variety of comfortable rooms with beautiful views of the sea. Amenities include free Wi-Fi, an on-site restaurant, and a bar. Guests can enjoy the lovely promenade that stretches along the coast, perfect for leisurely walks and exploring local shops and cafes. Prices typically range from €70 to €180 per night. The Sliema Marina Hotel is about a

30-minute taxi ride from Malta International Airport or accessible via public transport by taking a bus to Sliema. Reservations can be made through the hotel's website or through travel booking platforms.

For those seeking a hostel experience, The Wanderers Hostel in St. Julian's is an excellent choice. This modern hostel provides a range of accommodations, from dormitory beds to private rooms, making it suitable for solo travelers, groups, and families. The hostel features a communal kitchen, lounge areas, and organized social events, allowing guests to meet fellow travelers. Prices for dormitory beds typically range from €15 to €35 per night, while private rooms can cost between €50 and €100. The Wanderers Hostel is approximately a 25-minute drive from Malta International Airport. You can reach it by taxi or take a bus to St. Julian's and walk to the hostel. Booking can be done through the hostel's official website or popular hostel booking sites.

In addition to these recommended accommodations, there are many other hotels, guesthouses, and hostels throughout Malta that cater to various preferences and budgets. Whether you choose a luxury hotel with all the amenities or a cozy hostel that fosters a sense of community, you'll find plenty of options to suit your needs. It's advisable to book your accommodations in advance, especially during peak tourist seasons, to secure the best rates and availability. Many hotels and hostels offer flexible cancellation policies, making it easier to adjust your travel plans if necessary. By researching your options and considering your priorities, you can find the perfect place to stay that enhances your experience of this beautiful Mediterranean archipelago.

Safety Tips and Emergency Contacts

When visiting Malta, understanding safety tips and knowing emergency contacts can greatly enhance your travel experience and provide peace of mind. While Malta is generally considered a safe destination for tourists, it is still important to take precautions and be aware of your surroundings, just as you would in any other country. The Maltese people are known for their hospitality and friendliness, making it easy for visitors to feel welcome and secure. However, being informed about safety measures and emergency procedures is essential for any traveler.

One of the first safety tips is to stay vigilant, especially in crowded areas such as markets, tourist attractions, and public transportation. Pickpocketing can occur in busy places, so keep an eye on your belongings and ensure that bags and wallets are securely zipped and stored. It is advisable to carry only what you need for the day, leaving valuable items like passports and large amounts of cash in a safe location, such as your hotel safe. It is also wise to use a crossbody bag or a money belt that can be hidden under clothing to keep your items secure.

When it comes to transportation, Malta offers several options, including buses, taxis, and car rentals. Public buses are a reliable and cost-effective way to explore the islands, but be aware of your surroundings while traveling on public transport. If you choose to use taxis, opt for licensed taxi services or ride-hailing apps, which provide more security and transparency. For those planning to rent a car, familiarize yourself with local traffic laws and driving customs, as they may differ from those in your home country. Malta drives on the left side of the road, and road conditions can vary, so exercise caution, especially in rural areas where roads may be narrow or winding.

While exploring the beautiful Maltese coastline and its stunning beaches, it is essential to take care while swimming and engaging in water sports. Pay attention to any warning signs, especially regarding strong currents or dangerous areas. Lifeguards are present at many popular beaches, so always heed their advice. Additionally, it is important to stay hydrated and protect yourself from the sun, as Malta can get quite hot during the summer months. Applying sunscreen regularly and wearing appropriate clothing can help prevent sunburn and heat exhaustion.

If you find yourself in an emergency situation, it is crucial to know the local emergency numbers. In Malta, the emergency number for police, fire, and ambulance services is 112. This number is accessible from any phone and will connect you to the appropriate emergency service. English is widely spoken in Malta, so you should be able to communicate your situation effectively. It is also wise to keep a list of important contacts, such as your country's embassy or consulate, as well as your accommodation's contact information, in case you need assistance.

The nearest hospitals and medical facilities are available throughout the islands, with larger hospitals located in Valletta and Birkirkara. If you need medical assistance, you can visit a pharmacy, which can often provide basic first aid supplies and advice. For more serious issues, hospitals have English-speaking staff, and the healthcare system in Malta is generally well-regarded. Travelers are advised to have travel insurance that covers medical expenses, as this can provide added security and ease of mind.

While Malta is relatively safe, being aware of local customs and laws is equally important. Respect for local traditions and cultural practices will enhance your experience and ensure that you do not inadvertently offend anyone. For example, when visiting churches or religious sites, it is customary to dress modestly, covering shoulders and knees. Furthermore, drinking alcohol in public places may be restricted in some areas, especially during religious festivities, so it's important to be aware of local regulations.

Staying informed about current events and local news can also help you stay safe during your travels. Checking the weather forecast before engaging in outdoor activities is important, as sudden changes in weather can affect plans. It is also wise to follow any advisories or updates from local authorities, especially regarding safety or travel restrictions.

In case of theft or loss of personal belongings, report the incident to the local police as soon as possible. Keeping a record of your valuables, including serial numbers and photographs, can be helpful in case you need to file a report for your insurance. Your hotel can also assist you with contacting the police and may offer additional support in such situations.

Lastly, the Maltese are known for their friendliness and willingness to help. If you ever feel lost or in need of assistance, do not hesitate to ask locals for directions or advice. They will likely be more than happy to help you navigate the islands and ensure you have a pleasant experience. By staying aware of your surroundings, taking precautions, and knowing how to access emergency services, you can enjoy all that Malta has to offer while feeling safe and secure. This combination of preparation and awareness will allow you to fully immerse yourself in the rich culture, history, and beauty of this Mediterranean gem, ensuring that your visit is both enjoyable and worry-free.

Money Matters: Currency and Budgeting

When planning a trip to Malta, understanding money matters such as currency and budgeting is essential for a smooth and enjoyable experience. Malta uses the Euro (€) as its official currency. The Euro is widely accepted across the European Union, making it convenient for travelers coming from other Eurozone countries. For visitors arriving from outside Europe, it is important to exchange their home currency for Euros upon arrival. Currency exchange services are available at airports, banks, and exchange offices throughout the island. While exchanging currency, travelers should be aware of exchange rates, as they can vary. It is often a good idea to compare rates from different providers to get the best deal. Additionally, withdrawing cash from ATMs can be a convenient way to obtain Euros, and many ATMs accept international debit and credit cards.

In terms of the cost of living, Malta can be considered relatively affordable compared to other Mediterranean destinations, but prices can vary depending on location and the type of services. The cost of accommodation is one of the biggest expenses travelers will face. In popular tourist areas such as Valletta and St. Julian's, prices for hotels can be higher, especially during the peak season. However, visitors can find budget options, such as hostels or guesthouses, that offer good value. On average, travelers might spend anywhere from €50 to €300 per night for accommodations, depending on their preferences.

Food costs can also vary significantly. Eating out at restaurants can range from inexpensive local eateries where a meal might cost around €10 to €20 to more upscale dining options where a meal could exceed €50 or more. Maltese cuisine features local dishes that are delicious and often reasonably priced, especially in less touristy areas. For those looking to save money, purchasing groceries and preparing meals can be a cost-effective option. Supermarkets and local markets offer a wide range of fresh produce, meats, and other essentials at reasonable prices.

Transportation is another aspect of budgeting for a trip to Malta. Public transportation, particularly buses, is a convenient and affordable way to get around the islands. A single bus ticket typically costs around €1.50 to €2.00, depending on the time of day. Visitors can purchase a Tallinja Card, which offers discounted fares and is suitable for those planning to use public transport frequently. For those who prefer more flexibility, renting a car is another option, with prices varying based on the vehicle type and rental duration. Fuel prices are generally similar to those in other European countries, so budgeting for gasoline is also necessary if you choose to drive.

When it comes to payment methods, cash is widely accepted in Malta, but credit and debit cards are also commonly used. Most hotels, restaurants, shops, and attractions accept major credit cards like Visa and MasterCard. However, it is advisable to carry some cash, especially when visiting smaller towns or markets where card payment may not be available. Contactless payments are increasingly popular, making transactions quick and easy. It is also worth noting that some businesses may impose a minimum charge for card transactions, so carrying cash can help avoid any inconvenience.

For tourists, it is crucial to inform their bank of their travel plans to avoid any issues with card usage while abroad. Some banks may flag international transactions as suspicious and block the card, so notifying them ahead of time can ensure smooth access to funds during your trip. Additionally, consider checking for any foreign transaction fees associated with your credit or debit card. Some banks offer travel-friendly cards that do not charge these fees, which can save money during your travels.

CHAPTER 3

TOP ATTRACTIONS

Valletta: The Capital City

Valletta, the capital city of Malta, is a vibrant and historic destination that attracts visitors from around the world. Located on the southeastern coast of the island, Valletta is perched on a peninsula that separates the Grand Harbour from Marsamxett Harbour. Its strategic location has made it an important site throughout history, serving as a fortress city, a cultural hub, and a center for governance. Valletta was founded in 1566 by the Knights of St. John and is known for its well-preserved architecture, stunning views, and rich history. The city is a UNESCO World Heritage site and is often regarded as one of the most concentrated historic areas in the world.

Getting to Valletta is relatively straightforward, as it is well-connected by public transport and accessible from various parts of the island. If you arrive at Malta International Airport, the easiest way to reach Valletta is by taking a taxi, which takes approximately 20 minutes. Alternatively, you can use the public bus service, which offers several routes to Valletta from the airport. The bus journey might take a little longer, around 30 to 40 minutes, depending on traffic. For those staying in nearby towns such as Sliema or St. Julian's, regular ferries operate between these locations and Valletta, providing a scenic route across the water. Once in Valletta, the city is compact and walkable, allowing you to explore its narrow streets and historic sites with ease.

Valletta is packed with attractions that showcase its rich history and cultural heritage. One of the most iconic landmarks is St. John's Co-Cathedral, a stunning example of Baroque architecture. The exterior may seem understated, but inside, visitors are treated to a breathtaking display of ornate decorations, including intricate carvings, gilded ceilings, and beautiful frescoes. The cathedral houses the famous painting "The Beheading of Saint John the Baptist" by Caravaggio, which draws art lovers from around the globe. Exploring this cathedral provides insight into the religious significance of the Knights of St. John and the artistic achievements of the era.

Another must-visit site is the Grand Master's Palace, which served as the residence of the Grand Master of the Knights of St. John. Today, it is the seat of the Parliament of Malta and is open to the public. Visitors can tour the lavish state rooms, adorned with tapestries and portraits, and admire the impressive architecture. The palace's central courtyard is a peaceful spot to rest while soaking in the grandeur of this historic building. Nearby, the Upper Barracca Gardens offer stunning panoramic views of the Grand Harbour and the surrounding areas, making it an ideal location for a leisurely stroll. The gardens are beautifully landscaped, with fountains and benches that provide a serene escape from the bustling city.

For those interested in history, the National Museum of Archaeology is a treasure trove of artifacts that highlight Malta's rich prehistoric past. The museum showcases items from the Neolithic period, including pottery, statues, and tools. It provides context for Malta's ancient civilizations and their way of life, offering a fascinating glimpse into the island's history long before the arrival of the Knights. Visitors can learn about the Megalithic Temples of Malta and see the famous "Sleeping Lady" statue, one of the most significant finds from the prehistoric era.

Exploring Valletta's streets also leads to the historic Fort St. Elmo, which played a crucial role in Malta's defense. This star-shaped fortification offers exhibits about the Great Siege of 1565 and the military history of the island. Visitors can walk around the fort, enjoy the beautiful views of the sea, and gain insight into Malta's strategic importance throughout history. The fort is also home to the National War Museum, which contains a collection of weapons, uniforms, and artifacts that illustrate Malta's military heritage.

Valletta is also famous for its vibrant atmosphere, with many shops, cafes, and restaurants lining the streets. Strolling through the city allows visitors to experience local life and enjoy delicious Maltese cuisine. Try traditional dishes such as pastizzi, which are flaky pastries filled with ricotta or peas, or sample local seafood dishes at waterfront restaurants. Valletta has a lively café culture, making it a perfect place to relax with a coffee and watch the world go by.

One of the unique aspects of Valletta is its rich cultural scene. The city hosts various events, festivals, and performances throughout the year, celebrating everything from music and dance to food and art. The Valletta Baroque Festival, held every January, showcases classical music in stunning historic venues. The city also has several theatres, galleries, and cultural centers where visitors can experience local talent and creativity.

As the sun sets, Valletta transforms into a lively hub with bars and restaurants offering a vibrant nightlife. The atmosphere is particularly enjoyable in the warmer months when outdoor seating becomes popular. Enjoying a drink while overlooking the harbor as the city lights reflect off the water creates a memorable experience.

Valletta is a captivating destination that seamlessly blends history, culture, and modernity. Whether you are exploring its historic sites, enjoying the local cuisine, or immersing yourself in the vibrant atmosphere, Valletta offers countless opportunities for making lasting memories. With its rich heritage and stunning scenery, a visit to Valletta is sure to be a highlight of any trip to Malta.

Mdina: The Silent City

Mdina, often referred to as the "Silent City," is one of Malta's most captivating attractions, rich in history and charm. Located in the central part of the island, Mdina is perched on a hilltop, offering stunning views of the surrounding landscape. This ancient walled city served as the capital of Malta for centuries and is known for its well-preserved medieval architecture and narrow, winding streets. The city's tranquil atmosphere, combined with its historical significance, makes it a must-visit destination for tourists seeking to experience Malta's heritage.

Getting to Mdina is quite straightforward, and there are several options available for visitors. If you are arriving from Valletta, the capital city, you can take a direct bus that connects the two locations, with a journey time of approximately 30 minutes. The bus service is reliable and frequent, making it an easy and economical choice. For those who prefer a more scenic route, a taxi ride from Valletta to Mdina will take around 20 minutes. Alternatively, if you are staying in nearby areas such as Sliema or St. Julian's, you can also catch a bus to Valletta and then transfer to a bus heading to Mdina. Many visitors also opt to rent a car, which provides the flexibility to explore the surrounding countryside and other attractions at their own pace.

Once you arrive in Mdina, the first thing you will notice is its striking architecture. The city is surrounded by imposing walls that date back to the medieval period, and these fortifications create an air of mystery and history. Entering Mdina feels like stepping back in time, as the cobblestone streets are lined with beautiful palaces, quaint shops, and charming cafés. The atmosphere is peaceful, which is why it has earned the nickname "Silent City." There are very few vehicles allowed inside the city, allowing visitors to enjoy a leisurely stroll while taking in the sights.

One of the main attractions in Mdina is St. Paul's Cathedral, an exquisite example of Baroque architecture. The cathedral was built in the 17th century and features a stunning interior adorned with intricate frescoes, ornate altars, and beautiful woodwork. Visitors can admire the impressive dome and the artwork that tells the story of St. Paul, who is believed to have been shipwrecked on Malta in 60 AD. The cathedral also has a museum that showcases religious artifacts and historical items related to the church and the Knights of St. John.

Another significant site is the Mdina Dungeons, which offer a glimpse into the darker aspects of the city's history. Located in the old prison of Mdina, these dungeons are a fascinating attraction for those interested in the medieval period. Visitors can explore the dark corridors and chambers, which are filled with exhibits that detail the trials and punishments of that era. The experience can be quite immersive, making it a memorable visit for those interested in history.

Mdina is also home to the Palazzo Falson, a medieval house that has been transformed into a museum. This historic residence showcases a collection of art, furniture, and artifacts that reflect the lifestyle of the Maltese nobility over the centuries. The museum offers guided tours, allowing visitors to learn about the history of the building and its former inhabitants while enjoying stunning views from its rooftop terrace.

For those looking to relax and soak in the views, the Bastion Square offers a perfect spot to enjoy the picturesque scenery of the Maltese countryside and beyond. The square is located at the edge of the city walls and provides breathtaking views of the surrounding fields and villages. It is an excellent place to take photos or simply unwind in the serene atmosphere. There are benches where visitors can sit and enjoy the surroundings, making it a lovely spot for a break during your exploration of the city.

Food enthusiasts will also find delight in Mdina, as there are several cafés and restaurants offering traditional Maltese cuisine. Visitors can savor local dishes such as rabbit stew, pastizzi, and fresh seafood, often served in charming outdoor settings with views of the city. Many eateries feature locally sourced ingredients, allowing tourists to experience authentic Maltese flavors while enjoying the beautiful surroundings.

To make the experience even more memorable, tourists can take part in guided tours that explore the history and legends of Mdina. Several companies offer walking tours led by knowledgeable guides who can share fascinating stories about the city's past, including tales of knights, nobility, and the architectural evolution of the area. These tours often include visits to key attractions and provide a deeper understanding of the cultural significance of Mdina.

Overall, Mdina is a treasure trove of history, beauty, and tranquility. Its unique blend of historical significance, stunning architecture, and peaceful atmosphere makes it a must-visit destination for anyone traveling to Malta. Whether you are exploring its ancient streets, visiting its historical sites, or simply enjoying the views, Mdina offers an unforgettable experience that captures the essence of Malta's rich heritage. A trip to Mdina promises to be a highlight of your visit, allowing you to immerse yourself in the charm and history of this remarkable city.

Gozo Island: A Natural Paradise

Gozo Island, known for its stunning natural beauty and tranquil atmosphere, is a fantastic destination for those visiting Malta. Located approximately 5 kilometers northwest of the main island, Gozo is the second-largest island in the Maltese archipelago. It is known for its scenic landscapes, charming villages, and rich history, making it a popular getaway for tourists seeking a more relaxed experience compared to the bustling atmosphere of Malta's main island.

Getting to Gozo is quite simple. The most common way to reach the island is by taking a ferry from Cirkewwa, which is located at the northern tip of Malta. The ferry service operates frequently throughout the day, with a journey time of about 25 minutes. The ferry ride offers beautiful views of the coastline and the sea, making it an enjoyable part of the trip. Tickets can be purchased at the terminal, and it's advisable to check the ferry schedule in advance, especially during peak tourist seasons when the ferries can be busier. For those who prefer to drive, you can take your car on the ferry, which allows for greater flexibility in exploring the island upon arrival.

Once on Gozo, visitors are greeted by lush landscapes, rolling hills, and picturesque farmland, which are in stark contrast to the urban areas of Malta. The island is home to several charming villages, each with its own character and attractions. One of the most notable villages is Victoria, the capital of Gozo, which is also known as Rabat. Victoria features the impressive Citadel, a fortified city that offers panoramic views of the island. Exploring the narrow streets of Victoria, visitors can find local shops, cafes, and historic sites. The Citadel itself houses several museums, including the Gozo Museum of Archaeology, where you can learn about the island's rich history dating back to prehistoric times.

Another popular attraction on Gozo is the Azure Window, a natural limestone arch located near the village of Dwejra. Although the Azure Window collapsed in 2017, the area remains a stunning spot to visit, known for its breathtaking coastal views and crystal-clear waters. Nearby, the Dwejra Bay offers opportunities for swimming, snorkeling, and diving. The underwater world around Gozo is teeming with marine life, making it a favorite spot for divers of all levels. The nearby Blue Hole, a natural pool of seawater, is particularly popular among divers for its unique rock formations and vibrant underwater ecosystem.

For those interested in beaches, Gozo has several beautiful options to choose from. Ramla Bay is one of the most famous beaches on the island, known for its reddish-golden sand and calm waters. It is an excellent spot for sunbathing, swimming, and enjoying water sports. The beach is surrounded by scenic countryside, creating a picturesque setting for relaxation. Other popular beaches include Mgarr ix-Xini, a secluded cove perfect for swimming and kayaking, and Marsalforn Bay, a charming fishing village with a lovely beach and vibrant waterfront restaurants.

Gozo is also known for its traditional crafts and local products. Visitors can explore artisan shops and markets that sell handmade goods, including pottery, lace, and textiles. The island's farmers' markets offer fresh produce, local cheeses, and traditional Maltese sweets, providing a taste of Gozo's agricultural bounty. Taking the time to sample local delicacies is a great way to immerse yourself in the island's culture.

Cultural experiences abound on Gozo, with numerous festivals and events taking place throughout the year. The village of Xaghra is known for its annual festivals, where visitors can experience traditional music, dance, and food. The Feast of the Assumption, celebrated in August, is particularly lively, with processions and fireworks lighting up the night sky. These events provide a glimpse into the vibrant community spirit and traditions of the island.

For those who enjoy outdoor activities, Gozo offers plenty of opportunities for hiking and exploring nature. The island has a network of trails that lead through beautiful countryside, past ancient ruins, and along stunning coastal cliffs. The Ta' Cenc cliffs are a popular hiking destination, providing breathtaking views of the sea and surrounding landscape. Nature lovers will appreciate the chance to spot diverse wildlife, including various bird species that migrate through the area.

Accommodations on Gozo range from luxurious hotels to quaint bed-and-breakfasts and self-catering apartments, catering to various preferences and budgets. Many visitors opt for accommodations in or near Victoria for easy access to attractions, while others may choose to stay near the coast for beautiful sea views and a more relaxing atmosphere. The island is known for its hospitality, and many places offer personalized service, making your stay enjoyable.

Comino and the Blue Lagoon

Comino is a small island located between Malta and Gozo, known for its stunning natural beauty and crystal-clear waters. It is the third-largest island in the Maltese archipelago, covering an area of just 3.5 square kilometers. Despite its size, Comino is a popular destination for tourists, especially for those seeking a tranquil escape and breathtaking scenery. The island is famous for the Blue Lagoon, a picturesque bay with vibrant turquoise waters that attract visitors from all over the world.

Reaching Comino is quite simple, with several options available for travelers. The most common way to get to the island is by taking a ferry from either Malta or Gozo. If you are departing from Malta, ferries typically leave from Cirkewwa, which is located at the northern tip of the main island. The ferry ride to Comino takes about 25 minutes and provides stunning views of the surrounding sea and coastline. Alternatively, if you are coming from Gozo, there are also ferry services that connect directly to Comino. During the summer months, many boat operators offer day trips that include stops at the Blue Lagoon, making it easy to plan a visit.

Upon arrival at Comino, visitors are greeted by the island's serene atmosphere and stunning landscapes. The Blue Lagoon is undoubtedly the highlight of Comino, renowned for its calm, shallow waters that appear in vibrant shades of blue and green. This idyllic setting is perfect for swimming, snorkeling, and sunbathing. The lagoon is surrounded by rocky cliffs and sandy shores, providing a picturesque backdrop for relaxation. It is a popular spot for families, couples, and anyone looking to unwind in a beautiful natural environment. Visitors can rent sunbeds and umbrellas to enjoy a comfortable day by the water, and there are also a few kiosks where you can buy snacks and refreshments.

In addition to swimming, the Blue Lagoon offers excellent opportunities for snorkeling. The clear waters are home to a variety of marine life, including colorful fish and underwater plants. Many visitors bring their own snorkeling gear or rent equipment locally to explore the underwater world. The area around the lagoon is safe for snorkelers, making it suitable for both beginners and more experienced enthusiasts. Exploring the underwater landscape can be a memorable part of your trip to Comino.

For those who enjoy hiking and exploring, Comino has several walking trails that lead to beautiful viewpoints and secluded beaches. The island's rugged terrain is ideal for outdoor adventures, with paths that meander along the cliffs and through the natural landscape. One popular hiking route takes you to the top of the hill overlooking the Blue Lagoon, where you can enjoy breathtaking panoramic views of the sea and nearby islands. The tranquil environment and stunning scenery make for an unforgettable hiking experience.

Another notable attraction on Comino is the historic St. Mary's Tower, located on the eastern side of the island. This 17th-century watchtower was built by the Knights of St. John as a defense against pirates and invaders. Today, it stands as a testament to the island's history and offers a glimpse into the past. Visitors can explore the tower and enjoy the stunning views of the surrounding waters and coastline. The tower is a great spot for photography, especially during sunrise or sunset when the light casts beautiful colors across the landscape.

While Comino is known for its natural beauty, it is also a place of tranquility and peace. There are no major hotels or resorts on the island, making it a perfect getaway for those looking to escape the hustle and bustle of everyday life. Visitors can choose to spend a day on the island or stay overnight in a basic guesthouse. For those interested in a unique experience, camping on Comino is permitted in designated areas, allowing you to immerse yourself in nature and enjoy the sounds of the sea at night.

To make your experience even more memorable, consider taking a boat tour around the island. Many operators offer trips that include stops at hidden coves, sea caves, and other beautiful locations along the coastline. These tours often provide opportunities for swimming, snorkeling, and exploring areas that are less accessible by foot. Whether you choose a leisurely boat ride or an adventurous speedboat excursion, the views of Comino's cliffs and the surrounding waters are breathtaking.

The Megalithic Temples

The Megalithic Temples of Malta are among the oldest free-standing structures in the world and represent a significant aspect of the islands' rich cultural heritage. These remarkable sites date back to between 3600 BC and 2500 BC, making them older than Stonehenge and the Pyramids of Giza. The temples are located on the islands of Malta and Gozo, with several key sites that attract tourists eager to learn about ancient history and experience the grandeur of these monumental structures.

One of the most famous of these temples is the Ħaġar Qim temple complex, located on the southern coast of Malta, near the village of Qrendi. Ħaġar Qim is positioned on a hilltop overlooking the Mediterranean Sea, offering stunning views of the surrounding landscape. This UNESCO World Heritage site is easily accessible by car or bus from the capital city of Valletta, which is about 30 minutes away. Visitors can take a direct bus to the nearby village of Qrendi and then enjoy a short walk to the temple complex. The site is well signposted, making it easy for tourists to navigate.

Another significant site is the Mnajdra temple complex, located just a short walk from Ħaġar Qim. Mnajdra consists of three main temples built on a hillside and is noted for its remarkable architectural features, including intricate stonework and alignments with the sun. This site is also accessible by the same transportation methods as Ħaġar Qim, making it convenient to visit both locations in one trip.

For those traveling to Gozo, the Ggantija temples are a must-see attraction. Situated near the village of Xagħra, the Ggantija temples are considered some of the oldest religious structures still standing today. They are part of a UNESCO World Heritage site and are believed to have been built around 3600 BC. Getting to Gozo requires taking a ferry from Cirkewwa on Malta, which takes about 25 minutes, followed by a short bus or taxi ride to the temples.

Visiting the Megalithic Temples provides a unique opportunity to connect with Malta's ancient history. The temples are built from large limestone blocks, some weighing several tons, showcasing the impressive engineering skills of the prehistoric inhabitants. Each temple complex features a series of altars and stone chambers, believed to have been used for rituals and ceremonies. The layout of the temples is carefully designed, with some structures oriented toward the sun, suggesting that ancient builders had a deep understanding of astronomy.

At Ħaġar Qim, visitors can see a variety of archaeological features, including a large central altar and several smaller ones used for offerings. The stones are adorned with carvings and other symbols, adding to the mystique of the site. Information panels throughout the complex provide insights into the temple's history and significance, helping visitors understand its cultural context.

Mnajdra is famous for its breathtaking views and intricate carvings, as well as the remarkable preservation of its structures. The temples here are organized into three distinct areas, each featuring beautifully crafted stonework. The southern temple is especially noteworthy, with its main entrance designed to align with the sunrise during the equinoxes. This astronomical alignment indicates that the ancient builders held significant knowledge about the natural world around them.

The Ggantija temples on Gozo are equally impressive, featuring two main structures surrounded by a high stone wall. The larger temple, which is about 7,000 years old, has massive stone blocks that are remarkably well-preserved. The site also has a small museum that showcases artifacts discovered during excavations, including pottery and tools, providing further context to the lives of the people who built and used these temples.

In addition to exploring the temples themselves, visitors can enjoy a range of activities to enhance their experience.

Guided tours are available at all three temple sites, offering deeper insights into the history and significance of the structures. Local guides can share fascinating stories and facts that may not be readily available on information panels. Taking a guided tour can enrich your visit, allowing you to ask questions and engage more fully with the history of the sites.

Photography is also a popular activity at the Megalithic Temples, with the stunning landscapes and intricate stonework providing ample opportunities for memorable shots. Visitors are encouraged to capture the beauty of the temples and the surrounding scenery, particularly during the golden hours of sunrise and sunset when the light casts beautiful shadows and highlights the stones' textures.

For those interested in local culture, the nearby villages often host festivals and events that celebrate Malta's heritage. Participating in these activities can provide a more comprehensive understanding of how the ancient temples continue to influence modern Maltese culture. Local crafts, food, and traditions are often showcased at these events, allowing visitors to immerse themselves in the local way of life.

The Megalithic Temples of Malta offer a remarkable glimpse into the island's ancient past, showcasing impressive architecture and rich cultural heritage. With their strategic locations on both Malta and Gozo, these sites are easily accessible and provide a range of activities for visitors. From exploring the intricacies of the temple structures to enjoying guided tours and local festivities, a visit to the Megalithic Temples promises to be a memorable experience, allowing you to connect with the history and culture that have shaped Malta over thousands of years. Whether you are a history enthusiast, a nature lover, or simply looking for a unique travel experience, the Megalithic Temples are a must-see attraction that will leave a lasting impression.

CHAPTER 4

HIDDEN GEMS

Off the Beaten Path: Secret Beaches

Malta is renowned for its beautiful beaches, but beyond the popular spots like Golden Bay and Mellieħa Bay, the islands also boast a number of secret beaches that offer tranquility, stunning views, and a chance to escape the crowds. These hidden gems provide visitors with a unique opportunity to enjoy the natural beauty of Malta in a more peaceful setting. Exploring these off-the-beaten-path beaches can make for a memorable experience, filled with adventure and discovery.

One of the best-kept secrets is Fomm ir-Rih Beach, located on the northwest coast of Malta. This secluded beach is surrounded by cliffs and lush vegetation, providing a stunning backdrop for sunbathers and nature lovers alike. Getting to Fomm ir-Rih can be a bit challenging due to its remote location. Visitors typically drive to the nearest village of Baħar iċ-Ċagħaq and then follow a hiking trail down to the beach. The hike takes about 15 to 20 minutes and is worth the effort for the stunning views that await. Once there, you can enjoy the calm waters, ideal for swimming and snorkeling. The beach does not have facilities, so it is best to bring your own food and drinks. This makes it a perfect spot for a picnic while enjoying the peaceful surroundings.

Another hidden treasure is Paradise Bay, situated near the village of Għajnsielem on Gozo. Though more well-known than some other secret beaches, it still offers a quieter experience compared to Malta's more famous beaches. To reach Paradise Bay, you can take a ferry from Cirkewwa to Gozo, which takes about 25 minutes, followed by a short bus or taxi ride to the beach. The beach is small and sheltered, with soft golden sand and clear waters that are perfect for swimming and sunbathing. Visitors can also explore the nearby coves and enjoy a relaxing day by the sea. There are some facilities available, including sunbed rentals and a small café, making it a convenient choice for a day trip.

Qarraba Bay is another secret beach that should not be missed. Located near the village of St. Paul's Bay, Qarraba Bay is known for its striking landscape, with high cliffs framing the beach. Getting there requires a bit of effort, as visitors need to hike down a steep path from the cliffs above. The beach is less crowded than others, offering a peaceful environment for those looking to relax. The waters are crystal clear and great for swimming, and the surrounding area provides ample opportunities for exploration. Visitors should remember to bring water and snacks, as there are no facilities on the beach.

Għajn Tuffieħa Bay is yet another hidden gem worth visiting. Situated just a short distance from the more popular Golden Bay, this beach offers a quieter alternative with stunning natural surroundings. To get there, visitors can either walk along a scenic coastal path or take a short drive to the parking area nearby. The beach is surrounded by steep cliffs and rolling hills, making it a perfect spot for nature enthusiasts. The golden sand and clear waters make it ideal for swimming, and the area is also popular for hiking and enjoying picturesque sunsets. Facilities are limited, but there are some beach bars and cafés nearby, providing refreshments for a day in the sun.

Lastly, Armier Bay offers a unique experience for those seeking a more secluded beach setting. Located on the northern coast of Malta, Armier Bay is made up of two sandy beaches, which provide ample space for visitors to relax. The bay is known for its tranquil waters, making it perfect for swimming and sunbathing. Getting there is simple; visitors can take a bus from Mellieħa or drive directly to the area. There are some beach facilities available, including kiosks offering snacks and drinks, as well as areas for renting sunbeds and umbrellas.

When planning to visit these secret beaches, it's important to keep a few tips in mind to ensure a safe and enjoyable experience. First, make sure to check the weather before heading out, as conditions can change quickly, especially near the coast. It's best to choose a sunny day for beach activities to fully enjoy the experience. Additionally, bring plenty of water, sunscreen, and snacks, as some beaches have limited facilities. Comfortable footwear is recommended for hikes to reach more remote beaches, as some paths can be uneven or steep.

It is also wise to consider visiting these beaches during the shoulder seasons of spring or fall when the weather is still pleasant, and the crowds are fewer. Early mornings or late afternoons can be the best times to enjoy the beaches, as you can experience breathtaking sunrises or sunsets in a quieter atmosphere.

Malta's secret beaches offer visitors a chance to explore the natural beauty of the islands while escaping the more crowded tourist spots. Each hidden gem has its unique charm, from the stunning views at Fomm ir-Rih to the peaceful sands of Għajn Tuffieħa.

Quaint Villages to Explore

Exploring the quaint villages of Malta offers visitors a chance to experience the charm and authenticity of the islands beyond the typical tourist spots. Among the hidden gems are Marsaxlokk and Mellieħa, two villages that provide unique insights into Maltese culture and lifestyle. Each has its own distinct character, attractions, and activities, making them worthwhile destinations for anyone looking to delve deeper into Malta's rich heritage.

Marsaxlokk is a picturesque fishing village located on the southeastern coast of Malta, approximately 10 kilometers from Valletta. This charming village is easily accessible by bus, taxi, or even by car, with several bus routes connecting it to the capital and other major towns. The journey by bus takes about 30 minutes, and the scenic route offers beautiful views of the coastline. As you approach Marsaxlokk, the vibrant colors of the traditional fishing boats, known as "luzzu," come into view. These boats are often painted in bright hues of blue, yellow, and red, featuring the eye of Osiris, which is believed to protect fishermen at sea.

One of the main attractions in Marsaxlokk is its bustling fishing market, which takes place every Sunday morning. The market is a feast for the senses, filled with the sounds of local vendors, the smell of fresh seafood, and the sights of colorful stalls displaying an array of fish, fruits, and vegetables. Visitors can wander through the market, sampling local delicacies and engaging with the friendly vendors. Fresh catch from the sea is available, including local favorites like swordfish and octopus. This vibrant atmosphere allows you to experience the heart of the community and learn about traditional fishing practices that have been passed down through generations.

In addition to the market, Marsaxlokk offers a range of delightful waterfront restaurants and cafes where visitors can enjoy fresh seafood dishes while overlooking the harbor. Dining in one of these establishments provides a fantastic opportunity to taste traditional Maltese cuisine, such as fish soup or "bragioli," while soaking in the relaxed atmosphere of the village. For those interested in history, the village also has several historical sites, including the Church of Our Lady of Pompei, a beautiful Baroque church that overlooks the waterfront and features stunning artwork.

Beyond the fishing market and dining options, Marsaxlokk is also a great starting point for exploring the surrounding area. Visitors can take boat trips to nearby attractions, such as the Blue Grotto and the small island of Filfla. These boat tours offer a unique perspective of the coastline and an opportunity to see hidden caves and stunning rock formations. Snorkeling and diving are also popular activities in this area, allowing visitors to experience the rich marine life and underwater beauty of Malta.

Moving on to Mellieħa, located in the northern part of Malta, this village is known for its breathtaking views, rich history, and beautiful surroundings. Mellieħa is easily reachable by public transport, with frequent bus services from Valletta taking about 40 minutes. Visitors can also opt for a taxi or drive, with parking available in the village.

Mellieħa is perhaps best known for its stunning beach, Mellieħa Bay, which is the largest sandy beach in Malta. The bay is perfect for families, offering shallow waters ideal for swimming and sunbathing. There are also various water sports available, such as kayaking and paddleboarding. The beach is lined with cafes and restaurants, providing the perfect spot to relax and enjoy the beautiful Mediterranean views.

Aside from the beach, Mellieħa is rich in history and offers several interesting sites to explore. One significant landmark is the Mellieħa Sanctuary, a church dedicated to the Madonna. This beautiful church dates back to the 19th century and is located on a hill overlooking the village. The sanctuary is a pilgrimage site and features stunning artwork and a peaceful atmosphere, making it a great place to reflect and appreciate the local culture.

Another historical site in Mellieħa is the Red Tower, also known as the St. Agatha's Tower. This 17th-century watchtower was built by the Knights of St. John as a defense against pirates and invaders. Today, visitors can climb to the top of the tower for panoramic views of the surrounding countryside and coastline. Exploring the Red Tower provides insight into Malta's military history while offering an excellent photo opportunity.

For nature lovers, Mellieħa is surrounded by scenic countryside and offers numerous hiking trails that lead through beautiful landscapes. The area is known for its diverse flora and fauna, making it a fantastic spot for walking and enjoying the outdoors. The nearby Mellieħa Heights provides stunning views of the bay and is a popular area for photography, especially during sunrise and sunset.

Both Marsaxlokk and Mellieħa embody the charm of Malta's rural communities, offering visitors a chance to experience local life, culture, and history. Whether you're wandering through the bustling market in Marsaxlokk, enjoying fresh seafood by the harbor, relaxing on the sandy shores of Mellieħa Bay, or exploring historical landmarks, these quaint villages provide unforgettable experiences.

Local Markets and Artisanal Shops

Malta is a treasure trove of unique local markets and artisanal shops that showcase the island's rich culture, craftsmanship, and culinary delights. These hidden gems not only offer visitors a chance to find distinctive souvenirs but also provide an authentic glimpse into the daily lives of the Maltese people. Exploring these markets and shops can be an enriching experience, allowing travelers to connect with local traditions and support artisans who take pride in their work.

One of the most famous local markets in Malta is the Marsaxlokk Fish Market, held every Sunday morning in the charming fishing village of Marsaxlokk. Located on the southeastern coast of Malta, this market is easily accessible by public transport, with buses running frequently from Valletta and other towns. The journey takes about 30 minutes and offers scenic views of the coastline. As you stroll through the market, you will be greeted by an array of fresh fish and seafood, brought in by local fishermen. The vibrant atmosphere is filled with the sounds of vendors calling out their prices and the smell of the sea.

In addition to fresh seafood, the market features stalls selling local produce, cheeses, and various artisanal products. Visitors can taste local delicacies such as fresh octopus salad or fried calamari, providing a true taste of Maltese cuisine. The colorful fishing boats in the harbor create a picturesque backdrop, making it a perfect spot for photography. Exploring the market allows tourists to interact with friendly locals and gain insight into traditional fishing practices that have been passed down through generations.

Another hidden gem for local shopping is the Valletta Market, officially known as Is-Suq tal-Belt. This recently renovated market is located in the heart of Valletta and offers a variety of fresh produce, meats, cheeses, and artisanal goods. Visitors can wander through the market, sampling local treats and picking up unique souvenirs. The market is a great place to find Maltese specialties such as Ħobż biż-żejt (Maltese bread with oil and toppings), pastizzi (savory pastries), and various types of honey and jams made from local ingredients. The atmosphere is lively, with both locals and tourists enjoying the vibrant surroundings.

For those interested in handcrafted items, Mdina Glass is a must-visit destination. Located just outside the ancient walled city of Mdina, this glassblowing factory and showroom showcases exquisite glassware created by skilled artisans. Visitors can observe the glassblowing process and see how molten glass is transformed into beautiful pieces of art. The factory offers a wide selection of unique items, including vases, bowls, and jewelry, all handcrafted on-site. Purchasing a piece of Mdina Glass not only provides a beautiful souvenir but also supports local craftsmanship.

In addition to Mdina Glass, the Ta' Qali Crafts Village is an excellent spot for finding artisanal products. Located in the central region of Malta, Ta' Qali is a hub for local artisans and craftspeople. The village features numerous shops and workshops where visitors can browse handmade pottery, lace, leather goods, and jewelry. Many artisans are happy to share their stories and techniques, providing a deeper understanding of their craft. Ta' Qali is easily accessible by car or bus, making it a convenient destination for those looking to explore Malta's rich artisanal traditions.

Another unique market experience can be found at the Marsascala Market, held every Friday morning in the coastal town of Marsascala. This smaller market offers a more relaxed atmosphere, where visitors can find fresh produce, local fish, and various goods. The market is set near the picturesque harbor, making it a lovely spot to enjoy a leisurely morning while sampling local flavors and engaging with friendly vendors.

For a different shopping experience, the Sliema Promenade features a variety of boutique shops and local vendors selling handmade goods, clothing, and souvenirs. This vibrant area is a popular destination for both locals and tourists, offering a mix of shopping and scenic views of the Mediterranean. Walking along the promenade allows visitors to soak in the lively atmosphere while discovering unique shops and cafes.

When visiting these local markets and artisanal shops, it's important to keep a few tips in mind to enhance your experience. First, take your time to explore and interact with the vendors. Many are passionate about their products and enjoy sharing their stories and expertise. Sampling local foods is highly recommended, as it provides an authentic taste of Maltese culture. Don't be afraid to ask questions about the items you are interested in, as this can lead to interesting conversations and insights.

Bargaining is generally not common in Malta, as prices are often set; however, in some markets, a friendly conversation can sometimes lead to a discount, especially when purchasing multiple items. Cash is widely accepted, but it's wise to carry some euros, as not all vendors may accept credit cards. Always check for quality, especially when purchasing artisanal goods, to ensure you are getting a product that is well-made and worth the investment.

Malta's local markets and artisanal shops offer a wealth of opportunities for visitors to discover unique souvenirs and experience the island's vibrant culture. From the bustling Marsaxlokk Fish Market to the handcrafted treasures at

Mdina Glass and the lively atmosphere of Ta' Qali Crafts Village, these hidden gems provide insight into the local way of life. Exploring these markets not only allows travelers to find special items to take home but also supports local artisans and contributes to the preservation of traditional crafts. A visit to these markets and shops can create lasting memories and a deeper appreciation for Malta's rich heritage and culture.

Unforgettable Views: Hidden Lookouts

Malta, with its stunning landscapes and breathtaking coastline, offers a variety of hidden lookouts that provide unforgettable views, perfect for photography enthusiasts and nature lovers alike. These hidden gems are scattered across the islands, often tucked away from the more touristy spots, allowing visitors to capture the natural beauty of Malta in a tranquil setting. Each lookout offers a unique perspective of the landscape, whether it be dramatic cliffs, serene beaches, or charming villages, making them ideal locations for stunning photographs.

One of the most picturesque lookouts is the Fomm ir-Rih Viewpoint, located on the northwest coast of Malta. This scenic spot offers breathtaking views of the Mediterranean Sea and the rugged cliffs that define this part of the island. To reach Fomm ir-Rih, visitors can drive to the village of Baħar iċ-Ċagħaq and then follow a short hiking path down to the viewpoint. The hike takes approximately 15 minutes and leads you through lush vegetation and rocky terrain. Once at the viewpoint, you can capture stunning photos of the cliffs plunging into the deep blue sea, especially during sunrise or sunset when the colors of the sky create a magical backdrop. This area is also perfect for nature lovers, as it provides opportunities for birdwatching and exploring the diverse flora of the region.

Another remarkable lookout is the Ta' Cenc Cliffs, located on the southern coast of Gozo. The cliffs rise dramatically from the sea, offering some of the most spectacular views in Malta. The area is accessible by car, with ample parking available nearby. A short walk from the parking area leads you to the edge of the cliffs, where you can enjoy panoramic views of the ocean and the surrounding landscape. The cliffs are particularly impressive during the evening, as the setting sun casts warm hues over the sea and rocks, creating a perfect scene for photography. The Ta' Cenc area is also rich in history, with ancient cart ruts and the remains of prehistoric structures adding to its charm.

For those seeking a more urban perspective, the Upper Barracca Gardens in Valletta provide stunning views of the Grand Harbour and the Three Cities. The gardens are located near the historic center of Valletta and are easily accessible by foot or by bus. Visitors can enjoy a leisurely stroll through the beautifully landscaped gardens while taking in the breathtaking vistas of the harbor. The lookout point at the gardens is a fantastic spot for photographs, especially of the historic fortifications and the colorful boats in the harbor. The gardens are well-maintained and provide a peaceful oasis amidst the hustle and bustle of the city, making them a perfect place to relax and enjoy the scenery.

Another hidden lookout worth visiting is the Għajn Tuffieħa Bay Viewpoint, located near the village of Mellieħa. This spot offers breathtaking views of one of Malta's most beautiful beaches. To get there, visitors can drive or take a bus to Mellieħa and then follow a short path leading to the viewpoint. The lookout provides sweeping views of the golden sands and turquoise waters of Għajn Tuffieħa Bay, framed by rugged cliffs. This area is especially popular during the golden hours of sunrise and sunset, when the light creates stunning reflections on the water. The viewpoint also provides access to the beach below, where visitors can enjoy a day of sunbathing or swimming after capturing their perfect photos.

In Gozo, the Xlendi Bay Lookout offers a different yet equally captivating perspective. Xlendi is a small coastal village known for its picturesque bay surrounded by high cliffs. The lookout point can be reached by a short walk from the village, making it accessible for visitors. The bay is a great place for photography, particularly at dusk when the lights from the restaurants and homes reflect on the water. Visitors can also take a stroll along the promenade, where they can enjoy local cuisine in one of the waterfront restaurants while soaking in the view.

To make the most of your experience at these hidden lookouts, consider the following tips. First, plan your visit during the early morning or late afternoon to capture the best light for photography. The golden hour, shortly after sunrise and before sunset, provides the most flattering light and vibrant colors. Second, be prepared for changing weather conditions, as Malta's coastal areas can be windy and unpredictable. Wearing comfortable shoes and bringing water and snacks can enhance your enjoyment of the hikes to these viewpoints.

Additionally, it's a good idea to check local maps or ask for directions, as some lookouts may not be well signposted. Many visitors find that using a local guide or joining a photography tour can provide insights into the best spots and help discover other hidden gems along the way.

Malta is home to numerous hidden lookouts that offer unforgettable views and unique photography opportunities. From the rugged cliffs of Fomm ir-Rih to the serene beaches of Għajn Tuffieħa, these scenic spots allow visitors to appreciate the natural beauty and diverse landscapes of the islands. By taking the time to explore these hidden gems, travelers can create lasting memories and stunning images that capture the essence of Malta's charm. Whether you are a seasoned photographer or simply looking to enjoy the view, these lookouts promise a rewarding experience that showcases the breathtaking beauty of Malta.

CHAPTER 5

LOCAL INSIGHTS

Food and Drink: Must-Try Dishes

Malta's culinary landscape is a delightful reflection of its rich history and diverse cultural influences. Traditional Maltese cuisine is characterized by its use of fresh, local ingredients and recipes passed down through generations. As you explore the islands, you will encounter a variety of must-try dishes that showcase the flavors of Malta, as well as local wines and beers that perfectly complement these meals. Eating and drinking your way through Malta is not just about the food; it's an experience that connects you with the islands' traditions and people.

One of the quintessential Maltese dishes to try is Rabbit Stew or Fenkata, which is considered the national dish. The preparation typically involves marinating the rabbit in red wine, garlic, and herbs, then slow-cooking it until tender. The result is a rich, flavorful dish that embodies the essence of Maltese cooking. Many local restaurants serve this dish, particularly in villages like Mellieħa and Marsaxlokk, where traditional recipes are cherished. Eating rabbit stew is not just about tasting the food; it's about experiencing a dish that has historical significance and is often served during festive occasions. Pair it with a side of maltese bread and a glass of local red wine for a complete meal.

Another must-try dish is Bragioli, which consists of beef olives stuffed with a mixture of minced meat, herbs, and spices, simmered in a rich tomato sauce. This dish is typically served with mashed potatoes or vegetables, making it a hearty option. You can find Bragioli in various restaurants across Malta, but for an authentic experience, look for family-run establishments that pride themselves on traditional cooking methods.

No visit to Malta would be complete without trying Pastizzi, which are flaky pastries filled with either ricotta cheese or mushy peas. These delicious snacks are a popular street food and can be found at bakeries and kiosks throughout the islands. Try them fresh out of the oven for the best experience. The village of Sliema is particularly famous for its pastizzerias, where locals gather to enjoy these treats at all hours of the day.

If you're looking for something sweet, Kannoli is a traditional dessert that is also a must-try. These pastry shells are filled with sweetened ricotta cheese, often flavored with citrus zest and chocolate chips. You can find delicious Kannoli at various dessert shops, especially in Valletta and Mdina. The combination of the crispy shell and creamy filling makes for a delightful treat that encapsulates the flavors of Malta.

As you explore Malta's food scene, don't miss the opportunity to try local seafood dishes, which reflect the islands' coastal culture. Freshly caught fish, calamari, and shellfish are commonly featured on menus, often prepared simply with olive oil, lemon, and herbs to highlight the natural flavors. Marsaxlokk is renowned for its seafood restaurants, where you can enjoy a meal while overlooking the picturesque harbor filled with colorful fishing boats.

In addition to its traditional dishes, Malta boasts a thriving wine scene. The island's Mediterranean climate is ideal for viticulture, and several local wineries produce a variety of red, white, and rosé wines. One of the most well-known local wines is Meridiana, which is made from indigenous grape varieties. You can visit vineyards such as Meridiana Wine Estate and Delicata Winery for guided tours and tastings, allowing you to sample some of the best wines Malta has to offer. Pairing local wines with traditional Maltese dishes creates a delightful culinary experience that showcases the island's rich agricultural heritage.

Malta is also home to a growing craft beer scene. Breweries like Farsons Brewery, located in the heart of the island, produce a variety of beers, including lager, ales, and specialty brews. A visit to the brewery provides insight into the brewing process and allows you to sample their offerings in a welcoming setting. Trying local beers is a great way to complement your meals and discover unique flavors that are distinct to Malta.

When exploring local markets, visitors can find various artisanal products, including locally produced olive oil, honey, and traditional sweets. The Valletta Market, also known as Is-Suq tal-Belt, is a great place to find fresh ingredients, local cheeses, and baked goods. Many stalls offer samples, allowing you to taste before you buy, and the vibrant atmosphere adds to the experience of shopping for local products.

To truly immerse yourself in the Maltese food culture, consider participating in a cooking class or a food tour. Many local chefs offer hands-on experiences where you can learn to prepare traditional dishes using fresh, local ingredients. This not only enhances your culinary skills but also gives you a deeper appreciation for the history and culture behind Maltese cuisine.

Festivals and Events to Experience

Malta is a vibrant island rich in history and culture, and one of the best ways to experience this heritage is through its festivals and events. These celebrations reflect the island's traditions, customs, and communal spirit, offering visitors a unique glimpse into the Maltese way of life. Among the most notable events are the Maltese Carnival and various religious festivals, each providing a memorable experience filled with excitement, color, and local flavor.

The Maltese Carnival is one of the most anticipated events of the year, typically held in February, just before the start of Lent. The Carnival has deep roots in Maltese culture, dating back to the Middle Ages. It is celebrated across the islands, but the most spectacular festivities occur in Valletta and Floriana. The Carnival features vibrant parades with elaborate floats, costumed performers, and lively music, creating an electrifying atmosphere that captivates both locals and tourists.

To get to Valletta or Floriana during the Carnival, visitors can easily take a bus or taxi from various points on the island. The bus services run frequently, and the journey offers picturesque views of the coastline and cityscape. Once in Valletta, the main events typically take place in St. George's Square, where you can enjoy live performances, traditional dancing, and plenty of food stalls offering local treats. The energy of the Carnival is contagious, with both children and adults participating in the fun.

One of the highlights of the Carnival is the colorful costumes. Many participants spend months creating intricate outfits, often featuring masks and elaborate designs. Visitors are encouraged to join in the festivities, whether by dressing up in costumes or simply enjoying the vibrant atmosphere. Photography opportunities abound, with the stunning floats and lively performances providing perfect backdrops for memorable snapshots.

Another essential aspect of the Maltese Carnival is the traditional food that accompanies the festivities. Street vendors offer local delicacies such as frittura (fried snacks), kwarezimal (a traditional sweet made of flour and honey), and various pastries. Sampling these treats is a delightful way to immerse yourself in the local culture while celebrating alongside the community.

Religious festivals in Malta are also significant cultural events that showcase the island's rich heritage. With over 365 churches on the islands, it is no surprise that religious celebrations play a vital role in Maltese life. Each village has its own patron saint, and the feast day often includes processions, fireworks, and various festivities.

One of the most famous religious festivals is the Feast of St. Paul, celebrated in Valletta in February. This festival commemorates St. Paul's shipwreck on the islands in 60 AD, an event that holds great historical significance for the Maltese. The celebrations feature a grand procession with the statue of St. Paul being carried through the streets, accompanied by marching bands and traditional music. Visitors can easily reach Valletta by bus or taxi, and the atmosphere is filled with excitement, as locals come out to celebrate their patron saint.

Another prominent feast is the Feast of the Assumption in August, celebrated in various villages across Malta. The feast is particularly grand in Mellieħa, where the local church is adorned with flowers, and the streets are illuminated with colorful lights. The highlight of this festival is the evening procession, where a beautifully decorated statue of the Virgin Mary is paraded through the village. The air is filled with the sound of fireworks and the aroma of traditional foods being prepared in homes and stalls. Visitors can participate in the festivities, enjoying the local cuisine and witnessing the communal spirit of the celebration.

To truly immerse yourself in these festivals, it is recommended to check the local calendar of events and plan your visit accordingly. Each feast has its own unique charm, and participating in the local traditions can be a deeply enriching experience. In addition to the main events, many villages hold related activities such as fairs, concerts, and local markets, allowing visitors to explore the culture even further.

In conclusion, experiencing the Maltese Carnival and various religious festivals provides a fantastic opportunity to connect with the islands' culture and community. From the colorful and lively celebrations of the Carnival to the heartfelt traditions of religious feasts, these events showcase the vibrant spirit of Malta. Whether you are enjoying the elaborate parades, sampling local delicacies, or participating in the joyful atmosphere, attending these festivals will undoubtedly leave you with lasting memories of your time on the island. By venturing beyond the typical tourist attractions and engaging with local celebrations, you can gain a deeper appreciation for Malta's rich heritage and the warmth of its people.

Language and Customs

Common Phrases in Maltese

Maltese is a unique language that combines elements from various cultures and languages, reflecting the rich history of Malta. It is the only official Semitic language of the European Union and is derived primarily from Arabic, with influences from Italian, Sicilian, and English. Learning some common phrases in Maltese can greatly enhance your experience while visiting Malta, making interactions with locals more engaging and enjoyable. Understanding basic phrases will not only help in everyday situations but will also showcase respect for the local culture and people.

One of the first phrases that visitors will find useful is "Merħba," which means "Welcome." This is a friendly way to greet someone and is often used in shops, restaurants, and when entering someone's home. Another common greeting is "Bongu," meaning "Good morning," and "Bona sera," which translates to "Good evening." These greetings help establish a friendly rapport with locals and are appreciated when spoken in their native language.

When it comes to asking questions, "Kif inti?" means "How are you?" This phrase is a great way to initiate a conversation. In response, you can say "Bħalissa tajjeb, grazzi," meaning "I'm good, thank you." Understanding this exchange can lead to more in-depth discussions and connections with locals.

If you need assistance or want to ask for help, saying "Tista' tgħinni?" translates to "Can you help me?" This phrase is particularly useful when navigating new places or seeking information about local attractions. Additionally, if you wish to thank someone, you can say "Grazzi," which means "Thank you." It's always polite to show appreciation, and this simple word can go a long way in making a positive impression.

For those who enjoy trying local cuisine, learning how to order food can be very beneficial. When at a restaurant, you can ask for the menu by saying "L-iskeda tal-ikel, jekk jogħġbok," which means "The menu, please." If you want to order a drink, you can say "Nista' nġib x'ċajta?" meaning "Can I get something to drink?" This will help you navigate dining experiences more smoothly.

When making purchases, it is important to know how to ask for the price. The phrase "Kemm jiswa dan?" translates to "How much does this cost?" Understanding how to ask about prices will allow you to budget effectively and engage in conversations with shopkeepers. If you want to express that you are just looking, you can say "Ninsabu biss qed naraw," which means "We are just looking." This phrase can be helpful in shops where you don't want to feel pressured to make a purchase.

Another useful phrase is "Jien jien Maltin," meaning "I am Maltese," and it can be used humorously when locals mistake you for a local or to express appreciation for the culture. Understanding your origins or simply enjoying their company can create a warm atmosphere.

When bidding farewell, it is customary to say "Saħħa," meaning "Goodbye." You can also use "B'rispett" which means "Respectfully" as a more formal goodbye. Learning these parting phrases will leave a positive impression and reflect your willingness to connect with the culture.

Malta is known for its hospitality, and locals appreciate when visitors attempt to speak their language. This effort is often met with smiles and encouragement, making interactions warmer and more meaningful. Using common phrases not only aids in communication but also allows visitors to immerse themselves more deeply in the culture and environment of Malta.

In addition to conversational phrases, it is helpful to know some key vocabulary related to the local culture. For example, "Bajtar" means "Vegetable," and "Frott" translates to "Fruit." Knowing these words can enhance your experience at local markets, where fresh produce is abundant. You can also learn food-related phrases, such as

"Il-Ħobż" for "Bread" and "Ikel" for "Food," to enrich your culinary experiences while sampling Maltese delicacies.

When discussing transportation, you might hear or want to use "Karozza" for "Car" and "Buss" for "Bus." If you're inquiring about transportation, you can ask, "Kif niċċaqilqu?," which means "How do we get around?" This can be particularly useful when trying to navigate the public transport system or when looking for taxis.

Engaging with the locals and using these common phrases not only enhances your travel experience but also encourages meaningful connections with the Maltese people. Locals are typically very friendly and willing to help, and speaking their language can open doors to conversations and cultural exchanges that enrich your visit.

In conclusion, familiarizing yourself with common phrases in Maltese can significantly enhance your travel experience. The ability to greet locals, ask for help, order food, and express gratitude will not only make your interactions smoother but also show respect for the culture you are exploring. By embracing the language, you deepen your connection to the islands and the warmth of the Maltese community. Learning a few phrases can transform a simple vacation into an immersive cultural journey, allowing you to create lasting memories during your time in Malta.

Understanding Local Etiquette

Understanding local etiquette is essential for any traveler wanting to connect authentically with the culture and people of a destination. Malta, with its rich history and diverse influences, has its own set of customs and practices that visitors should be aware of to ensure a respectful and enjoyable experience. Being familiar with these local etiquette guidelines not only helps you navigate social interactions smoothly but also enhances your overall travel experience.

When greeting people in Malta, a friendly handshake is the most common form of introduction. This is typically accompanied by a warm smile, as Maltese people are known for their hospitality. In more familiar settings or among friends, a kiss on both cheeks is a common practice, starting with the left cheek. If you are in a formal situation, addressing individuals with their titles, such as "Mr." or "Mrs.," followed by their surname is polite. As you become acquainted with locals, using their first names is generally acceptable and often appreciated.

When visiting someone's home, it is customary to bring a small gift as a token of appreciation. This could be a box of sweets, flowers, or a bottle of wine. It shows respect and gratitude for their hospitality. Upon entering a Maltese home, it is polite to greet everyone present, and you should wait for the host to invite you to sit down. Also, taking off your shoes when entering someone's home is considered a sign of respect, although this may vary by household.

During meals, Maltese dining etiquette is somewhat relaxed, but there are still customs to observe. If you are invited to a traditional Maltese meal, it is customary to wait for the host to begin eating before you start. The host may offer a prayer or a toast, and it is polite to acknowledge it. When dining out, it is common for the waiter to bring bread to the table, which is often enjoyed with the meal. In Malta, it is common to ask for the bill at the end of the meal rather than having it presented automatically. Tipping is appreciated but not mandatory; rounding up the bill or leaving a small tip is generally seen as a nice gesture.

In terms of dress, Malta has a relatively casual approach, but it is always best to dress modestly, especially when visiting religious sites. The Maltese people take pride in their appearance, so wearing neat and clean clothes is advisable. When visiting churches or places of worship, men should avoid wearing shorts, and women should ensure their shoulders and knees are covered. This respect for religious customs is important to the local culture.

Malta is predominantly Roman Catholic, and many festivals and public holidays are centered around religious events. Being aware of these occasions can enhance your experience. For instance, during local feasts, it is common to see processions, fireworks, and celebrations in the streets.

Visitors are welcome to join in the festivities, but it is essential to be respectful of the traditions and customs being observed.

When interacting with locals, engaging in friendly conversation is common. Maltese people enjoy discussing various topics, including family, food, and local culture. Showing genuine interest in their customs and traditions is appreciated and can lead to more meaningful interactions. However, it is wise to avoid sensitive topics such as politics or religion unless you are familiar with the individuals and feel comfortable discussing such matters.

While public displays of affection are generally accepted in Malta, it is important to be mindful of your surroundings and the cultural context. Maltese people tend to be warm and affectionate, but keeping interactions respectful in public spaces is always a good practice. In contrast, discussions about personal matters may be viewed as intrusive if the relationship is not well established.

When it comes to transportation, be aware of local customs when using public transport. Buses are a popular mode of transport, and it is customary to allow passengers to disembark before boarding. Always give up your seat to elderly individuals, pregnant women, or anyone who appears to need it. If you are driving in Malta, remember that the roads can be narrow, and parking may be limited in certain areas. Observing traffic rules and being courteous to other drivers is important.

Photography is a wonderful way to capture memories during your trip, but it's essential to ask for permission before photographing individuals, especially in more private or religious settings. Many locals are happy to have their pictures taken, but a simple request shows respect for their personal space and privacy.

In shops and markets, it's common to greet the shopkeeper with a simple "Merħba" (welcome) when entering. Haggling is generally acceptable in markets, but it should be done politely. Always express your gratitude with a "Grazzi" (thank you) when making a purchase.

Finally, when attending events, festivals, or public gatherings, be respectful of the customs being observed. Joining in with enthusiasm while being aware of the underlying traditions will help you blend in with the locals and enhance your experience. Whether you are enjoying a traditional Maltese feast during a local festival or simply chatting with locals at a café, being mindful of etiquette will go a long way in making your visit to Malta enjoyable and fulfilling.

In summary, understanding local etiquette in Malta is key to a rewarding experience. From greetings and dining customs to respecting religious practices and engaging in conversation, being aware of these customs allows you to connect meaningfully with the Maltese people and their culture. Embracing local traditions not only enriches your travels but also fosters goodwill and positive interactions with the welcoming community you will encounter on this beautiful island. Whether you are indulging in the delicious local cuisine, exploring quaint villages, or celebrating at vibrant festivals, a respectful approach will help you create lasting memories during your time in Malta.

CHAPTER 6

MALTA FOR DIFFERENT TRAVELERS

Malta for Solo Tourists

Malta is an enchanting destination that offers a wealth of experiences for solo tourists, making it an ideal place for those who want to explore at their own pace. This small archipelago in the Mediterranean Sea is rich in history, culture, and stunning landscapes, providing a perfect blend of adventure and relaxation for independent travelers. With its warm climate, friendly locals, and relatively compact size, Malta is easy to navigate, making it suitable for solo exploration.

When planning a trip to Malta, solo travelers will find various transportation options to suit their needs. The public bus system is reliable and affordable, providing extensive coverage across the main island of Malta and its sister island, Gozo. Buses run frequently, making it easy to visit popular attractions, such as Valletta, Mdina, and the beautiful beaches along the coast. For those who prefer more flexibility, renting a bicycle or a scooter can be a great way to explore the island at your own pace. Malta is also pedestrian-friendly in many areas, particularly in cities like

Valletta and Sliema, where walking is a pleasant way to discover charming streets and local shops.

One of the main draws for solo tourists in Malta is its rich history. The islands are home to some of the oldest structures in the world, including the megalithic temples that predate Stonehenge and the Pyramids of Giza. Visiting these archaeological sites, such as Ħaġar Qim, Mnajdra, and Ggantija on Gozo, can be a profound experience. The temples provide insight into Malta's prehistoric cultures and are often less crowded than other tourist spots, allowing for a reflective atmosphere. Solo travelers can take their time to appreciate the intricate stonework and the beautiful surroundings.

In addition to archaeological wonders, Malta offers stunning natural beauty. The coastline is dotted with hidden coves and pristine beaches that are perfect for relaxing or swimming. Some of the best spots for solo travelers to enjoy include Golden Bay, Għajn Tuffieħa, and the Blue Lagoon on Comino. These locations not only offer beautiful scenery but also the opportunity to connect with nature. Spending a day at the beach can be a rejuvenating experience, providing a peaceful environment to unwind and reflect.

For those interested in local culture, visiting traditional markets and local festivals can provide unique insights into the Maltese way of life. The Marsaxlokk Fish Market on Sundays is a bustling hub of activity where solo travelers can sample fresh seafood, mingle with locals, and soak in the vibrant atmosphere. Engaging with local vendors and tasting traditional dishes can be a delightful way to immerse oneself in Maltese culture. Additionally, many villages celebrate their patron saints with colorful festivals throughout the year, offering a chance to experience lively processions, music, and local delicacies.

Maltese cuisine is another highlight for solo travelers, featuring a delicious mix of Mediterranean flavors and traditional dishes. Trying local specialties such as rabbit stew (Fenkata), pastizzi (flaky pastries filled with ricotta or peas), and Ħobż biż-żejt (Maltese bread with oil and toppings) is a must. Exploring local eateries and trying street food can be a fantastic way to savor the flavors of Malta while meeting fellow travelers and locals alike.

While Malta is generally safe for solo tourists, it's always important to remain vigilant and take basic safety precautions. The islands have a low crime rate, but like any tourist destination, petty theft can occur. It is advisable to keep personal belongings secure, especially in crowded areas or public transport. Solo travelers should also be mindful of their surroundings, particularly when exploring less-populated areas or venturing out at night. Most towns are well-lit and safe, but it's best to stick to main roads and avoid isolated paths after dark.

The warmth of the Maltese people adds to the appeal of traveling alone in Malta. Locals are known for their hospitality and friendliness, often willing to help tourists with directions or recommendations. Engaging in conversations with residents can lead to meaningful interactions and insights into local life. Joining group tours or classes, such as cooking or diving courses, can also be a great way to meet other travelers and make connections while exploring the island.

In terms of accommodation, Malta offers a wide range of options suitable for solo travelers, from budget hostels to luxurious hotels. Many hostels provide a friendly atmosphere where guests can meet fellow travelers, share experiences, and even join group activities. Guesthouses and boutique hotels in scenic locations offer more privacy while still providing opportunities to engage with other guests. Choosing accommodations in central areas, such as Valletta, Sliema, or St. Julian's, can enhance your experience by placing you close to attractions, restaurants, and nightlife.

The vibrant nightlife in Malta is also an attraction for solo tourists. Areas like St. Julian's, particularly the Paceville district, are known for their lively bars and clubs. While enjoying the nightlife, it's important to remain aware of your surroundings and stay with friends or in groups whenever possible. Many venues have friendly atmospheres where you can meet new people and enjoy live music or entertainment.

Malta is also home to numerous cultural events throughout the year, including art exhibitions, concerts, and theater performances. Attending local events can provide an enriching experience, allowing solo travelers to engage with the local arts scene and meet like-minded individuals. Keeping an eye on local event calendars can help you discover performances or festivals happening during your visit.

Malta is an excellent destination for solo travelers, offering a rich tapestry of history, culture, and natural beauty. The islands are easy to navigate, with a range of transportation options that make exploring hassle-free. From the ancient temples and stunning beaches to the vibrant markets and delicious cuisine, there is no shortage of activities to enjoy. By embracing the local customs, engaging with residents, and exploring the hidden gems of Malta, solo tourists can create lasting memories and enjoy a fulfilling travel experience. Whether you seek adventure, relaxation, or cultural immersion, Malta has something to offer every independent traveler.

Malta for Couples

Malta is a captivating destination that offers an abundance of experiences perfect for couples seeking a romantic getaway. With its stunning landscapes, rich history, and vibrant culture, Malta provides a unique backdrop for creating lasting memories together. Whether you're celebrating an anniversary, honeymooning, or simply looking to reconnect, the island has a variety of activities and sights to enjoy as a couple.

One of the most appealing aspects of Malta is its diverse and beautiful scenery. The island is blessed with dramatic coastlines, charming villages, and historic landmarks. Exploring these sights together can be a wonderful way to bond and create shared experiences. A visit to the Blue Lagoon on Comino is an ideal starting point. This small island, known for its crystal-clear turquoise waters, is accessible by a short ferry ride from Malta or Gozo. Couples can spend the day relaxing on the beach, swimming, and snorkeling in the warm waters. The serene environment is perfect for unwinding and enjoying each other's company, away from the hustle and bustle of everyday life.

After a day at the beach, consider taking a boat tour around the coastline. Many operators offer sunset cruises that provide breathtaking views of the Maltese landscape as the sun sets over the Mediterranean. These tours often include food and drinks, creating a romantic atmosphere where you can enjoy a meal while watching the sky change colors. A sunset sail is not only beautiful but also a wonderful opportunity for couples to connect and appreciate the magic of the moment.

For couples who enjoy history and culture, visiting the ancient city of Mdina, also known as the "Silent City," is a must. This fortified city, which once served as the capital of Malta, is filled with narrow, winding streets, stunning architecture, and a sense of tranquility. Exploring Mdina together can feel like stepping back in time. You can visit St. Paul's Cathedral, which boasts impressive Baroque architecture, and wander through the quiet streets, stopping at charming cafes for a coffee or dessert. The panoramic views from the Bastion provide a perfect photo opportunity and a chance to share a romantic moment as you look out over the island.

Valletta, the capital city, is another fantastic destination for couples. The city is a UNESCO World Heritage site known for its stunning architecture and rich history. You can stroll hand-in-hand along the Valletta Waterfront, which is lined with colorful cafes and restaurants. Dining together at one of the waterfront establishments while enjoying views of the Grand Harbour can be a delightful experience. Consider trying local dishes, such as rabbit stew or seafood, for an authentic taste of Maltese cuisine.

In Valletta, the Upper Barracca Gardens offer a serene escape from the city's hustle. This beautifully landscaped garden features lovely paths and stunning views of the harbor and the Three Cities. It's an excellent spot for couples to relax, take in the scenery, and enjoy a peaceful moment together. The gardens are especially romantic during the late afternoon when the light casts a golden hue over the surroundings.

For a more adventurous experience, couples can explore the Blue Grotto, a series of sea caves located on the southern coast of Malta. A boat tour of the grotto allows you to witness the stunning natural beauty of the caves and the vibrant blue waters. You can swim in some areas, making it a fun and exhilarating activity to share. The stunning colors of the water and the surrounding cliffs create a romantic and picturesque setting that is perfect for couples looking to connect with nature.

Wine lovers will also appreciate the local wine scene in Malta. The island produces excellent wines, and many vineyards offer tours and tastings. Visiting a local winery can be a fun and romantic activity. You can learn about the wine-making process, explore the vineyards, and enjoy sampling a variety of wines. Many vineyards have beautiful settings, providing a scenic backdrop for a leisurely afternoon spent together.

For those looking for a unique experience, consider attending one of Malta's many festivals or events. The island hosts numerous celebrations throughout the year, from vibrant carnivals to religious feasts. Participating in these local events allows couples to immerse themselves in Maltese culture and create unforgettable memories. For example, the Feast of St. Paul in Valletta features lively processions, music, and delicious food, making it a joyful experience to share.

When it comes to accommodations, Malta offers a range of options that cater to couples. From luxurious hotels with stunning sea views to quaint boutique guesthouses, you can find the perfect place to stay. Many hotels offer romantic packages, including candlelit dinners, spa treatments, and private balconies. Choosing accommodation in central areas like Valletta or St. Julian's allows easy access to attractions and nightlife, making it convenient for couples who want to explore.

As the sun sets, Malta comes alive with nightlife options. St. Julian's is known for its vibrant nightlife, with numerous bars and clubs where couples can enjoy music, dancing, and cocktails. Whether you prefer a lively club scene or a more laid-back bar atmosphere, you will find plenty of options to suit your mood. Enjoying a night out together can add an extra layer of excitement to your trip.

Finally, a trip to Malta wouldn't be complete without spending some quiet moments at the beach. The island has many beautiful beaches, each offering a unique experience. Golden Bay and Għajn Tuffieħa are popular choices for their stunning sunsets and serene atmosphere. Relaxing on the sand, taking a swim in the clear waters, or simply enjoying each other's company by the sea can create lasting memories.

In conclusion, Malta is an idyllic destination for couples, offering a perfect blend of romance, adventure, and cultural experiences. With its beautiful landscapes, rich history, and welcoming atmosphere, the island provides countless opportunities for couples to connect and create unforgettable memories. From exploring charming cities and indulging in local cuisine to enjoying stunning views and participating in lively festivals, Malta has something for every couple to enjoy. By immersing yourselves in the local culture and embracing the experiences that the islands have to offer, you can ensure a romantic and memorable getaway that will be cherished for years to come.

Malta for Families

Malta is a wonderful destination for families looking to create lasting memories while exploring a beautiful and culturally rich environment. With its stunning landscapes, fascinating history, and numerous activities designed for all ages, Malta offers a diverse range of experiences that cater to family needs. Traveling with children can be both rewarding and challenging, but Malta's family-friendly atmosphere makes it easier to enjoy a vacation that appeals to everyone in the group.

One of the greatest advantages of visiting Malta as a family is the ease of getting around. The public transportation system, including buses, is reliable and affordable, making it convenient to access various attractions across the islands. Families can purchase a weekly bus pass that allows unlimited travel, which is an economical option for those planning to explore multiple locations. The compact size of Malta means that many attractions are within short distances of each other, which is ideal for families with young children who may not want to spend too much time traveling.

When it comes to family-friendly activities, Malta has a plethora of options to choose from. One of the most popular spots is the Popeye Village, located in the north of Malta. Originally built as a film set for the 1980 musical "Popeye," this colorful village has been transformed into a fun-filled amusement park. Families can enjoy interactive shows, rides, and even a chance to meet characters from the beloved film. Children can play on the beach or take part in water sports, while parents can relax and enjoy the beautiful surroundings. The village also features various food stalls and shops, making it a convenient place for families to spend a full day of fun.

Another fantastic destination for families is Aquarium in Qawra, which offers an engaging and educational experience for children of all ages. The aquarium showcases a wide variety of marine life native to the Mediterranean Sea, including colorful fish, sea turtles, and even sharks. Kids can learn about the importance of marine conservation through interactive exhibits and presentations. The aquarium also features a touch pool, allowing children to interact with marine creatures safely, making it an exciting and memorable experience.

For those interested in outdoor activities, the Malta National Aquarium is located near the beautiful coastline and provides opportunities for swimming and relaxing at nearby beaches. Families can spend a day at one of Malta's many sandy beaches, such as Mellieħa Bay or Golden Bay, which offer shallow waters and soft sands, making them ideal for children. Many beaches have amenities like sunbeds, umbrellas, and nearby restaurants that cater to families.

In addition to beach activities, Malta boasts a variety of historical sites that can be both educational and enjoyable for families. The ancient walled city of Mdina is a great place to explore with children. Known as the "Silent City," Mdina is filled with narrow streets and beautiful architecture that captivates visitors of all ages. Families can wander through the city, visiting attractions like the Mdina Cathedral and enjoying the panoramic views from the city walls. The rich history of Mdina can spark children's imaginations and inspire curiosity about Malta's past.

For a more adventurous experience, families can take a boat trip to the Blue Lagoon on Comino. This stunning location is famous for its crystal-clear waters and is perfect for swimming and snorkeling. Many boat operators offer family-friendly packages that include equipment rentals and refreshments. Spending a day at the Blue Lagoon is a wonderful way for families to bond while enjoying the natural beauty of the Maltese islands.

As families explore Malta, they can also take advantage of its numerous parks and recreational areas. The San Anton Gardens, located near Attard, is a beautiful public garden featuring lush greenery, fountains, and playgrounds. Families can relax under the shade of trees, have a picnic, or let their children play in the dedicated play areas. Another great spot for outdoor fun is the Argotti Botanic Gardens in Floriana, which features diverse plant species and tranquil walking paths, providing a serene environment for families to enjoy.

When it comes to dining, Malta offers a variety of family-friendly restaurants that cater to different tastes and budgets. Traditional Maltese cuisine includes dishes that appeal to children, such as pasta, pizza, and fresh seafood. Many restaurants offer kid-friendly menus, ensuring that even the pickiest eaters will find something they enjoy. Dining al fresco in the warm Mediterranean evenings can create a lovely atmosphere for families to unwind and reflect on their day's adventures.

Malta's local culture is also family-oriented, with many festivals and events throughout the year that celebrate traditions and community spirit. Participating in local celebrations can be a fun way for families to engage with the culture. Events such as the Maltese Carnival, held in February, are filled with colorful parades, costumes, and lively music, making it an exciting experience for children and adults alike. Many villages host their own feasts throughout the year, complete with fireworks, traditional food stalls, and games, providing opportunities for families to celebrate together.

Finally, safety is an important consideration for families traveling abroad. Malta is known for its low crime rate and is generally considered a safe destination for tourists, including families. Nevertheless, it is always wise to take basic precautions. Keeping an eye on children in crowded areas and teaching them about safety, such as staying close and not wandering off, can help ensure a worry-free experience.

In summary, Malta is an excellent destination for families, offering a diverse range of activities that cater to both adults and children. With its rich history, beautiful landscapes, and family-friendly attractions, Malta provides countless opportunities for families to bond and create cherished memories. From exciting adventures at amusement parks and historical sites to relaxing days on the beach, Malta promises a fulfilling and enjoyable experience for families of all sizes. By embracing the local culture and exploring the island's hidden gems, families can enjoy a vacation that combines fun, education, and unforgettable moments.

Malata for Groups

Malta is an ideal destination for groups seeking a mix of culture, adventure, and relaxation. With its rich history, stunning landscapes, and diverse range of activities, the islands offer something for everyone, making it perfect for family reunions, school trips, corporate retreats, or gatherings of friends. The compact size of Malta allows groups to easily explore its many attractions, ensuring that everyone can enjoy a memorable experience together.

One of the primary advantages of visiting Malta as a group is the ease of transportation. The public bus system is extensive and affordable, making it simple for groups to navigate between various attractions. Buses connect major cities and tourist sites, and purchasing group tickets can often lead to further savings. For those preferring a more private experience, renting a van or booking a guided tour can provide flexibility and convenience, allowing groups to tailor their itinerary to suit their interests.

When it comes to attractions, Malta is filled with historical sites and cultural landmarks that can be both educational and entertaining for groups. One must-visit location is Valletta, the capital city and a UNESCO World Heritage site. The city is rich in history, with impressive fortifications, beautiful churches, and vibrant streets. Groups can explore attractions like the Upper Barracca Gardens, which offer stunning views of the Grand Harbour, and the St. John's Co-Cathedral, renowned for its Baroque architecture and exquisite artwork. Guided tours can enhance the experience, providing insights into the history and significance of these sites.

Another significant historical site is Mdina, known as the "Silent City." This fortified medieval town offers a fascinating glimpse into Malta's past. Groups can wander through its narrow streets, visit the Mdina Cathedral, and enjoy panoramic views from the city walls. The calm atmosphere of Mdina allows for leisurely exploration, making it an excellent stop for groups looking to soak in the local culture. For larger groups, arranging a guided tour can provide a more structured experience, ensuring that everyone has the opportunity to learn about the rich history of the area.

For those interested in the outdoors, Malta offers a range of natural attractions perfect for group activities. The Blue Lagoon on Comino is a popular destination known for its stunning turquoise waters. Groups can take a ferry from Malta or Gozo to reach the lagoon, where they can enjoy swimming, snorkeling, and sunbathing. The surrounding area is perfect for picnics and relaxation, allowing groups to spend quality time together while taking in the beautiful scenery. It is advisable to visit during the off-peak times to avoid large crowds, ensuring a more enjoyable experience for everyone.

The Maltese countryside also offers beautiful hiking trails, such as the path leading to the Dingli Cliffs, which are the highest points on the island. This area is ideal for groups looking to enjoy nature and breathtaking views of the coastline. The cliffs offer several walking routes that can accommodate different fitness levels, making it suitable for everyone in the group. Bring along a picnic to enjoy at the top while taking in the stunning scenery of the Mediterranean Sea.

Groups can also take advantage of Malta's rich culinary scene, which provides numerous opportunities for shared dining experiences. Local cuisine is a highlight of any visit, and there are many restaurants that can accommodate groups. Enjoy traditional Maltese dishes such as rabbit stew, pastizzi, and fresh seafood. Some restaurants offer group menus, allowing for a tasting experience that showcases a variety of local flavors. Dining together is a great way to bond and enjoy the culinary culture of Malta, and many establishments have outdoor seating that enhances the experience.

For a unique and entertaining experience, consider arranging a traditional cooking class for your group. Many local chefs offer hands-on classes where participants can learn to prepare authentic Maltese dishes. This interactive experience not only provides a fun activity for the group but also allows everyone to learn about local ingredients and cooking techniques. At the end of the class, the group can sit down together to enjoy the fruits of their labor, creating a memorable shared meal.

When it comes to accommodations, Malta offers a wide range of options suitable for groups. From hotels with spacious family rooms to villas that can accommodate larger gatherings, there are plenty of choices to suit different budgets and preferences. Many hotels provide amenities such as swimming pools, restaurants, and activity planning services, making them convenient for groups. Additionally, renting a villa can provide a home-like atmosphere where groups can relax and enjoy each other's company after a day of exploring.

In terms of entertainment, Malta has a vibrant nightlife that can be appealing for groups looking to unwind after a day of sightseeing. Areas such as St. Julian's and Paceville are known for their lively bars and clubs. Group bookings are often available for nightlife experiences, including VIP packages or guided bar tours, allowing everyone to enjoy the evening without the stress of planning.

For those interested in cultural events, Malta hosts numerous festivals throughout the year, offering unique experiences for groups. The Maltese Carnival in February is a vibrant celebration featuring colorful parades, costumes, and performances. Participating in local festivals provides groups with the chance to engage with the community, experience traditional music, and enjoy local delicacies.

Visiting during the summer months also allows groups to enjoy various open-air concerts and events that showcase local and international talent. Checking local event calendars can help groups plan their visit around exciting happenings, providing opportunities for memorable experiences.

In summary, Malta is a fantastic destination for groups, offering a variety of activities that cater to different interests. The combination of rich history, beautiful landscapes, and vibrant culture ensures that every member of the group can find something enjoyable to experience. Whether exploring historical sites, enjoying nature, indulging in local cuisine, or participating in cultural events, Malta provides the perfect setting for groups to bond and create lasting memories together. With careful planning and a sense of adventure, groups visiting Malta will leave with a deeper appreciation for the islands and the unique experiences they offer.

CHAPTER 7

USEFUL INFORMATION

Useful Applications for Tourists in Malta

Traveling to Malta can be an exciting adventure, and having the right applications on your smartphone can greatly enhance your experience. With a range of useful apps available, tourists can easily navigate the islands, discover attractions, find dining options, and stay connected. Here is a detailed overview of some of the most valuable applications for tourists visiting Malta.

One of the first apps to consider is Google Maps. This application is essential for navigation, providing accurate directions for walking, driving, and public transport. Malta's public bus system is comprehensive, and Google Maps can help you find the nearest bus stop, view real-time schedules, and plan your journey. Whether you are heading to popular attractions like Valletta or the beaches in Mellieħa, having Google Maps at your fingertips will make it easy to explore the islands confidently.

For those interested in public transportation, the Malta Public Transport app is a must-have. This app provides detailed information on bus routes, schedules, and fares. You can purchase bus tickets directly through the app, which is convenient and allows you to avoid long lines at ticket booths. The app also features a journey planner that helps you determine the best routes to take based on your location and destination. This is particularly useful for families or groups traveling together, as it simplifies the process of navigating the public transport system.

When it comes to finding accommodations, the Booking.com app is an excellent resource. It offers a wide range of options, from hotels and guesthouses to hostels and apartments. You can filter your search based on price, location, and amenities to find the perfect place to stay. The app provides user reviews and ratings, which can help you make informed decisions. Additionally, you can access last-minute deals and flexible cancellation policies, making it a reliable option for travelers looking for accommodation in Malta.

Another valuable app for finding places to eat is TripAdvisor. This app is popular among travelers for its extensive database of restaurants, cafes, and bars. You can browse reviews, view photos, and check ratings to find the best dining options that suit your taste and budget. The app also allows you to filter your search by cuisine type, distance, and price range. Whether you're looking for traditional Maltese dishes or international cuisine, TripAdvisor will help you discover the local food scene.

For those interested in history and culture, the Maltese Heritage app is a fantastic resource. It provides information on historical sites, museums, and cultural landmarks throughout the islands. You can explore the history of Malta through detailed descriptions, photographs, and audio guides. This app is particularly useful for tourists visiting places like Mdina or the megalithic temples, as it enhances your understanding of the significance of these sites. The app often includes walking tours that guide you through different areas, ensuring you don't miss any hidden gems.

If you're looking to engage with the local nightlife, the Eventbrite app is helpful for discovering events, concerts, and parties happening in Malta. This app allows you to search for activities based on your interests and offers ticket purchasing options. Whether you want to enjoy live music in a bar or attend a cultural festival, Eventbrite provides a comprehensive overview of what's happening on the island during your stay. It's a great way to immerse yourself in the local scene and connect with other travelers and locals.

Staying connected while traveling is important, and the WhatsApp app is essential for communication. This messaging service allows you to keep in touch with family and friends back home or coordinate with your travel companions. Using WhatsApp for messaging and calling over Wi-Fi can help you save on international phone charges. You can also join group chats to keep everyone informed about plans and activities during your trip.

For those interested in outdoor activities, the Komoot app is an excellent tool for planning hiking and biking routes. Malta offers beautiful trails and paths, particularly around the countryside and coastal areas. Komoot provides detailed maps, route descriptions, and elevation profiles, making it easy to choose suitable paths based on your fitness level. The app also allows you to download maps for offline use, ensuring you can navigate even in areas with limited mobile data coverage.

If you want to dive into the vibrant local market scene, the Facebook Marketplace app can help you find local crafts and products. This platform allows you to connect with local artisans and vendors who sell handmade goods, unique souvenirs, and fresh produce. Shopping from local markets not only supports the community but also provides an authentic experience of Maltese culture. You can find information on local events, fairs, and craft markets, allowing you to discover one-of-a-kind items that reflect your trip to Malta.

For health and safety, especially in light of ongoing global concerns, the My Health Passport app can provide useful information regarding health services and COVID-19 regulations in Malta. This app can help you locate nearby clinics, hospitals, and pharmacies in case of emergencies. Additionally, it often contains updates on health protocols, testing sites, and vaccination information, ensuring you stay informed during your travels.

Finally, for families traveling with children, the Family Locator app can provide peace of mind. This app allows you to track family members' locations and communicate easily, which is particularly useful in crowded areas or busy attractions. Keeping everyone connected can enhance the experience, allowing you to explore the islands without worrying about losing track of each other.

In conclusion, having the right applications on your smartphone can significantly enhance your experience while visiting Malta. From navigating the public transportation system and finding great places to eat to discovering historical sites and enjoying local events, these apps provide valuable assistance for tourists. By leveraging technology, you can make the most of your trip, ensuring you create lasting memories while exploring this beautiful Mediterranean destination. Whether you are interested in history, cuisine, outdoor adventures, or cultural experiences, the right apps can help you navigate and enjoy all that Malta has to offer.

Tourist Information centers in Malta

Tourist information centers play a crucial role in enhancing the travel experience for visitors to Malta. These centers are strategically located across the islands, providing valuable resources, assistance, and local insights that help tourists navigate their surroundings and make the most of their visit. With a wealth of information at their fingertips, travelers can access maps, brochures, and expert advice on various attractions, accommodations, dining options, and activities that suit their interests and needs.

One of the primary tourist information centers is located in Valletta, the capital city of Malta. Situated near the main entrance to the city, this center serves as an excellent starting point for visitors arriving in Malta. The staff at the Valletta Tourist Information Center are knowledgeable and friendly, ready to assist tourists with questions about the city and the surrounding areas. They can provide detailed maps highlighting important landmarks, historical sites, and recommended walking routes. Additionally, the center offers brochures in multiple languages, showcasing various attractions and activities throughout Malta and Gozo.

In Valletta, tourists can inquire about guided tours, transportation options, and local events. The staff can recommend cultural experiences, such as visiting the Upper Barracca Gardens or exploring St. John's Co-Cathedral, and can help arrange bookings for guided tours, ensuring that visitors have a comprehensive understanding of Malta's rich history. The center also provides information on local restaurants and cafes, allowing tourists to find dining options that cater to their tastes and preferences.

Another important tourist information center is located in Sliema, a popular coastal resort town known for its shopping, dining, and picturesque promenade. This center caters to tourists looking to enjoy the beach, explore the nearby areas, or take ferry rides to Valletta. The Sliema Tourist Information Center offers similar services to those in Valletta, including maps, brochures, and personal recommendations. It also provides insights into water sports and other recreational activities available along the coastline, making it an excellent resource for families and adventure seekers.

The Mellieħa Tourist Information Center is another key location for tourists. Located near the stunning beaches of Mellieħa Bay, this center serves visitors who are primarily interested in enjoying Malta's natural beauty and outdoor activities. The staff can provide information about local attractions, including Popeye Village, the Mellieħa Sanctuary, and nearby hiking trails. Tourists can also learn about boat trips to the nearby Blue Lagoon on Comino and other islands. The Mellieħa center is particularly useful for those looking to enjoy a day at the beach or partake in family-friendly activities.

In Gozo, the sister island of Malta, the Victoria Tourist Information Center is an essential resource for visitors. Located in the capital city of Victoria (Rabat), this center provides information specific to Gozo, highlighting its unique attractions, such as the Azure Window, Dwejra Bay, and the ancient Ggantija Temples, which are among the oldest freestanding structures in the world. The knowledgeable staff at this center can assist tourists in planning their itinerary, recommending the best ways to explore the island, whether by rental car, bike, or on foot. They can also provide guidance on local customs, festivals, and cultural events happening during your visit.

In addition to offering maps and brochures, tourist information centers in Malta often provide free Wi-Fi, making it convenient for travelers to stay connected while planning their day. Many centers also have computers available for use, allowing visitors to research attractions or book tickets online. Some tourist centers even have small gift shops, where visitors can purchase local handicrafts, souvenirs, and Maltese products, supporting local artisans and bringing home a piece of Malta.

Tourist information centers also play a vital role in promoting local events and festivals. Malta hosts numerous cultural events throughout the year, from the colorful Carnival celebrations to religious feasts and concerts. By checking in at a tourist information center, visitors can find out about events happening during their stay, allowing them to participate in local traditions and experiences. This connection to the local culture enriches the overall travel experience and fosters a sense of community among visitors and residents alike.

Safety is another essential aspect that tourist information centers address. The staff can provide information about local customs and safety tips, helping tourists navigate their stay with confidence. They can inform visitors about common scams to watch out for, safe areas to explore, and emergency contact information. This support is particularly beneficial for solo travelers or families who may have specific concerns.

While most tourist information centers are open year-round, hours may vary depending on the season. It is a good idea to check in advance or visit their websites to confirm hours of operation and any special services they might offer. During peak tourist seasons, centers may host special events, such as guided walking tours or workshops, providing visitors with even more opportunities to engage with the local culture.

In conclusion, tourist information centers in Malta are invaluable resources for visitors looking to explore the islands. With knowledgeable staff, comprehensive information, and a welcoming atmosphere, these centers help tourists make the most of their time in Malta. From obtaining maps and brochures to receiving personalized recommendations and insights into local culture, these centers serve as essential hubs for planning and enjoying a successful trip. By visiting a tourist information center upon arrival, travelers can set the stage for a memorable and enriching experience, discovering all that Malta has to offer.

CONCLUSION

As we conclude this journey through Malta, we hope this guide has illuminated the many wonders that this beautiful archipelago has to offer. From its rich history and vibrant culture to stunning landscapes and delectable cuisine, Malta is a destination that caters to all types of travelers—families, couples, solo adventurers, and groups alike.

Throughout the pages of this book, we have explored the essential attractions and hidden gems, providing insights that will help you navigate the islands with confidence. We have highlighted the importance of embracing local customs, engaging with the welcoming Maltese people, and immersing yourself in the unique experiences available. Whether you are savoring the flavors of traditional dishes, wandering through ancient cities, or relaxing on picturesque beaches, every moment spent in Malta is an opportunity for discovery and connection.

We encourage you to step outside your comfort zone and explore the unexpected. Take the time to converse with locals, try new activities, and participate in cultural events. The warmth of the Maltese people, combined with the rich tapestry of history and nature, will create lasting memories that you will cherish long after your visit.

As you plan your trip, remember that Malta's charm lies not only in its iconic landmarks but also in the everyday moments that unfold during your stay. Whether it's enjoying a quiet sunset by the sea, laughing over a shared meal, or simply wandering through the vibrant streets, these experiences are what make travel truly enriching.

We wish you a wonderful adventure in Malta, filled with exploration, relaxation, and meaningful connections. May this guide serve as your companion, helping you uncover the beauty and magic of this remarkable destination. Safe travels, and may your journey through Malta be as unforgettable as the islands themselves.

Printed in Great Britain
by Amazon